SUPPLY TEACHERS'
SURVIVAL GUIDE

SUPPLY TEACHERS' SURVIVAL GUIDE

Glen Segell

Trentham Books

Stoke on Trent, UK and Sterling, USA

Trentham Books Limited

Westview House	22883 Quicksilver Drive
734 London Road	Sterling
Oakhill	VA 20166-2012
Stoke on Trent	USA
Staffordshire	
England ST4 5NP	

© Glen Segell 2003

ISBN 1 85856 281 3

Designed and typeset by Trentham Print Design Ltd., Chester and printed in Great Britain by Cromwell Press Ltd., Wiltshire.

Contents

Supply Teacher's Survival Guide

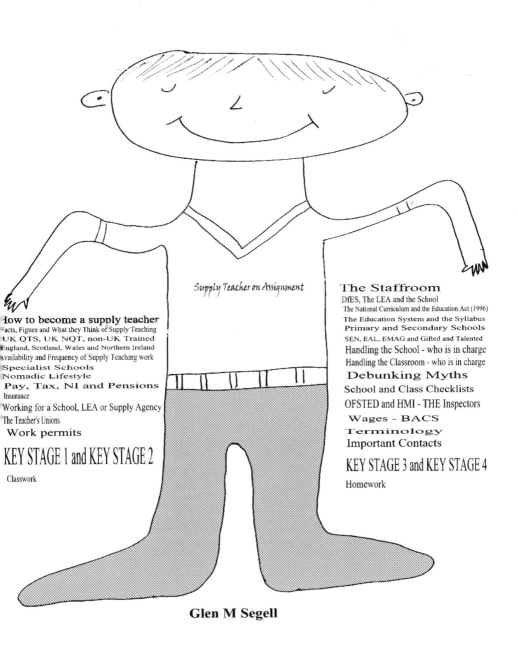

Supply Teacher on Assignment

The Staffroom
DfES, The LEA and the School
The National Curriculum and the Education Act (1996)
The Education System and the Syllabus
Primary and Secondary Schools
SEN, EAL, EMAG and Gifted and Talented
Handling the School - who is in charge
Handling the Classroom - who is in charge
Debunking Myths
School and Class Checklists
OFSTED and HMI - THE Inspectors
Wages - BACS
Terminology
Important Contacts

KEY STAGE 3 and KEY STAGE 4
Homework

How to become a supply teacher
Facts, Figues and What they Think of Supply Teaching
UK QTS, UK NQT, non-UK Trained
England, Scotland, Wales and Northern Ireland
Availability and Frequency of Supply Teaching work
Specialist Schools
Nomadic Lifestyle
Pay, Tax, NI and Pensions
Insurance
Working for a School, LEA or Supply Agency
The Teacher's Unions
Work permits

KEY STAGE 1 and KEY STAGE 2
Classwork

Glen M Segell

Preface

The highest form of charity is education. It is giving to someone so that the individual may be able to help him or herself. No matter the wages of a supply teacher, which are less than a teacher on contract with a school, there is always a rewarding feeling of achievement to see a child succeeding in gaining knowledge and the ability to utilize that knowledge. This is the case even if you are just teaching at a school for a single day.

This survival guide concentrates on the practicalities before, during and after an assignment of supply teaching. It offers insights and guidance, and is a comprehensive handbook for supply teachers in the United Kingdom as well as an essential guide for supply teachers when on the job. The aim of the book is to indicate questions to ask and points to look out for. It is not intended to provide specific information on individual supply agencies, local education authorities (LEA) or schools as no one specific employer can be recommended because each and every supply teacher is unique in his or her needs. This survival guide is a stepping-stone to your success as a supply teacher on which children's happiness and education might well depend.

The book started when I commenced work as a supply teacher years ago. I trust my experience to giving education to children in over 60 schools over the last four years will be supplemented through this survival guide to educate supply teachers. DfES has promised a series of publications for supply teachers that include five books, which I hope will be published sooner rather than later.

The notion to convert this experience to publishable format came on a Saturday afternoon session at the Educational Writers Group of the Society of Authors.

The book is dedicated to the children of London's schools, where I taught as a supply teacher, who showed me the respect that inspired me to pass on my experience to future supply teachers.

1

The difference between supply teaching and a regular post

'A day in the life of a supply teacher' begins with the sound of the alarm clock going off at 5:30 a.m. The supply rises from bed, sinks into the hot bathtub or dashes for the cold shower. After the ritual of cleansing yesterday's school, the supply dresses. The male supply dresses in suit and tie, and the female supply wears nice clothes – no jeans, no sneakers and no T-shirts for either. The supply prepares a paper bag lunch. There is no way of knowing whether school meals will be available or edible to your fancy or whether there will be food purchasing facilities near the school.

Halfway through preparing this lunch, the supply is interrupted by a phone call. The voice on the other end of the line, belongs to 'The Consultant' from the supply agency or the Local Education Authority (LEA). Sometimes this happens the night beforehand but changes do happen at the last minute. The consultant murmurs down the line 'I have School X, General Cover, no work prepared, one day supply assignment – will you take it?' You accept promptly and hang up the phone.

The supply day has begun: today you will be a maths teacher or maybe a geography teacher or maybe a PE teacher – general cover means jack of all trades, master of none. General cover means the regular teacher just called in sick so you will have to prepare work yourself in the half hour between arriving at school and the first lesson. The students need to be learning and you are their teacher for the day. Such is the daily supply teacher's life. You will only accept long term supply if it is your speciality subject and if there are good reasons for not going on contract directly with a school – the job is the same, but the obligations and pay are different.

Around the country, over 20,000 other supply teachers are doing the same as you are. You are unique in your needs but by deciding to work as a supply teacher, you have joined a growing number of professionals attracted by the freedom and flexibility offered by this career option. As a supply teacher you decide when and where to work while expanding your range of hands-on experience, and confidently developing your long term career. Supply teaching is not restricted to teachers trained in the UK – those with Qualified Teacher Status (QTS) – seeking a three day working week while tending the garden for two days, or those with young children who wish to spend more time with their own rather than other people's children. Supply teaching also offers newly trained teachers (NQT) as well as those returning to the profession the opportunity to experience a variety of schools before deciding on a permanent post. It also offers non-UK trained teachers a unique working-holiday opportunity.

Never, in my experience, has the choice and variety been better for those who have chosen teaching as a career and supply teaching as a career option. Many professional journals, newspapers, the internet and even the Yellow Pages carry large advertisements enticing qualified teachers into the world of supply teaching. The pay can be good if negotiated from the onset and the work is challenging. There is, nevertheless, a basic contradiction between the difficult roles that short term supply teachers are expected to fulfil, and the lack of support available to them in this situation. It is hardly surprising that some supply teachers find the job excessively difficult, giving rise to management's concerns over the quality of students' experience at their hands. To blame the unsatisfactory situation entirely on the supply teacher's inadequacies is hardly fair, and ignores the employer's responsibility to offer constructive professional development and support. The most awkward problem is how best to offer support to a supply teacher whose piecemeal-type work pattern does not allow easy access to school-based support systems and professional development. This survival guide is my answer.

New Labour, the Third Way and supply teachers

The reason why supply teaching has flourished as the heart of educational Public-Private-Partnership has its roots in Tony Blair's 1997 election mantra 'education, education, education' which is at the core of the New Labour's Third Way scheme. So it is no surprise that the government accepts the proliferation of private supply teachers agencies and supply teachers in state school classrooms. After transportation and SEN provisions, supply teaching is the largest single private sector involvement in schools. This has given supply agencies the status of education providers at the heart of state schools. Lack of direct government regulation and more flexible working practices give private supply agencies an advantage over LEAs, and this is likely to persist. Although some LEAs are trying to reintroduce their supply pools, Public Private Partnerships appear the more realistic way forward. Alternatives will be hard to find given the shortage of UK trained teachers – in 2001-2002 this was over 10,000 teachers nationwide. This does not mean that alternatives to supply teachers should not be explored should the system lose direction, especially if the National Curriculum is not being followed.

Supply teaching was a response to a crisis situation. The rise of the supply teacher system is a classic example of unintended education policies. Economic circumstances and societal changes created consequences which together precipitated a shortage of teachers for LEA supply pools. The long term future of supply teaching is not certain but it will fill a gap until government direction and popular support become geared to alternatives.

Supply teaching is not a career in its own right but is a current work option for qualified teachers. Supply teaching is not ideal. It is likely in the short term to further exacerbate shortages in the permanent teaching sector, and might significantly compromise children's education. Alternatives are being suggested to the currently predominant use of supply teacher agencies. These include:

- [ ] Using teaching émigrés as education consultants
- [ ] Having Ofsted Inspectors and union officials supply teach for at least one day in five, or half a term in six

☐ Restructuring when and how continuing professional development is carried out

☐ Developing effective use of new technologies as an alternative to emergency daily cover supply teachers

☐ Training so that staff without Qualified Teacher Status be used effectively as emergency cover

☐ Using support staff in classrooms and considering a specific separate qualification that would also form a pathway towards Qualified Teacher Status.

Supply teaching could thus be destined to move away from providing emergency cover for absent teachers to becoming a stepping stone for classroom assistants rather than a short term 'opt-out'. Students, who always need to be learning, will not be confronted with new faces each day in the form of supply teachers but will be supervised by support staff regularly seen and known in their school.

The government's response in the short term is to expand the number of training places for teachers. It tries to plug gaps by targeting specific groups. For example, the July 2002 Budget initiatives extended the golden hellos to secondary school teachers of English, Maths and Science. It is too soon to say whether these inducements will be enough to turn the tide. Under-funding of the public sector is commonly associated with a collapsing physical infrastructure but the lack of qualified and motivated workers who make up the human infrastructure may be harder to remedy than a shortage of buildings or equipment.

Policies and practices to improve the status and quality of supply teachers and a drive towards better recruitment and retention of contract teachers could eventually reduce the need for supply teachers. However, this is unlikely to happen soon as training of new teachers to Qualified Teachers Status takes two to four years. Government moves slowly. Meanwhile, supply teaching and supply teachers agencies will continue to provide a secure source for schools on a daily basis or even for term-long vacancies. Many supply teachers are performing daily miracles in continuing the learning process for the children who need it most. The use of supply teachers seems to be here to stay for the foreseeable future.

Why you would want to be a supply teacher and why a school needs you

A headteacher knows that the students need to be learning, and must find a teacher if there is an absence. A school needs you, the supply teacher, on a long term basis because an advertised vacancy has not been filled or because a teacher has gone on maternity leave, or gone sick for a prolonged period. A school needs you, the supply teacher, on a short term basis, because there is INSET or a teacher has gone sick on that day or is on a development course or is off-site for any reason.

Such eventualities give you, the supply teacher, options to going on a contract with a school. For many newly qualified teachers a full-time post will be the right step but you may be considering moving to a new area or would just like an opportunity to explore a number of schools before committing to a particular post. If this is your situation then working as a supply teacher can be the answer. You have the opportunity to build on your achievements and consolidate the skills you have acquired during your training. It is equally important that you have the opportunity to complete your induction period in an environment where you can receive the support, monitoring and assessment you require. If you work on one placement for a term or more this will form part of your induction period. The school in which you are working will be able to access Standards Fund support from the LEA to provide for your induction programme. Under current regulations you are permitted to split your induction year into separate one-term assignments in three different schools. You are also permitted to work for up to four terms on casual day-to-day supply while looking for a permanent post. After four terms you must be in a teaching post where you can commence induction.

Non-UK trained teachers on a working holiday or immigrating to Britain are advised not to dive directly into the deep end of a long term contract with a school. Supply on a daily basis gives such qualified teachers the ability to adjust to the British education system and to children's attitudes towards non-UK teachers. Every teacher will need a different period of adjustment. This supply will normally be for teachers off sick, teachers off for in-service educational training (INSET) or other unforeseen circumstances where a school is in a need of a few extra hands for a day or two. You can build this up to longer assignments as time goes on and you feel more confident, such as six weeks maternity cover or one full term due to teacher's unexpected illness or leaving. Some non-UK trained teachers however will prefer to continue daily cover for a few days a week while travelling. Current legislation permits a non-UK trained teacher to teach as a supply teacher for a maximum of four years without attaining qualified teacher status (QTS). There is also a limitation to how long can be spent at one school because the school as a government employer is obligated to advertise a teacher vacancy. Do not expect to do more than twelve weeks at the outset on long term supply for any specific school where the maximum is two consecutive terms.

Supply teaching is not just for NQTs and non-UK trained teachers. In 60 schools over four years I have also met the following: soon-to-be mothers who only wish to teach one or two days a week; mothers with young children who want a similar work-load; retired teachers who still wish to help the local community rather than tend gardens; nuns and priests who believe education is an act of charity; temporary resident poets and authors giving workshops; bored millionaires; consultants from supply teaching agencies moonlighting to keep their hand in on the other side of the telephone; cricket, football, and rugby coaches who are out of season for their main job; resting actors and musicians; un-employed carpenters and authors researching textbooks and survival guides.

What it means to become a supply teacher

Supply teaching differs dramatically from regular teaching in adminis-tration formalities, relations with colleagues, preparation of material, style of teaching and marking and examination procedures. In addition, there are the supply teacher's relations with the agency or the LEA over and above the school day. Supply teaching is distinctly different from a full-time teaching position but it can be a rewarding long term career.

Supply agencies, LEAs and schools all provide substantial advertising in big letters on why you should apply to work for them and, in small letters, the terms and conditions that apply. The gap occurs at the next step. None of the supply agencies, LEAs or schools provide in-depth guidance on what to do once the supply teacher is in the school and the classroom. Occasionally you might be given a two-page handout on arrival at a school on everything under the sun, including a map of the school, times of the daily programme, disciplinary procedures, telephone numbers of senior management and who you will cover. Perhaps by break time you might have the time to read this briefing – but that will probably be too late. Some supply agencies offer a form of mentoring but this is not the same as having advice before you start the assignment. More often than not, this mentoring is more to calm your nerves in a ten-minute telephone conversation than to provide substantial professional development. Some agencies and LEAs do offer afternoon or day long professional development courses, but this is after you have already commenced supply work and constitute large audiences on generic topics such as SEN, conversion from secondary to primary and behavioural management issues.

The lack of practical daily support is understandable considering that placement of a supply teacher to a school is normally by telephone through a supply agency consultant who sometimes has in excess of 200 requests per day for assignment placements, usually between school closing time circa 3:30 p.m. and 6 p.m. when supply teachers wish to spend time with their families. With such lack of crucial support supply teachers and even more so supply agencies invoke a range of responses from the downright angry to the strongly approving.

It is recognised that filling the gaps in schools and colleges with supply teachers, especially on a short term basis, is not ideal for the students or the permanent staff. Good and bad accounts abound from teachers, schools, LEAs and supply agencies. Anger stems from many sides because of the manner in which some supply agencies charge exorbitant rates to schools that pay teachers a modest wage. This anger is also directed at the government, since supply teachers are not eligible to pay contributions to the Teacher's Pension Scheme (TPS).

The approval comes from other teachers and schools. Teachers, like anyone else, have the right to decide when the disadvantages outweigh the benefits of freedom to work as and when they want and to concentrate on teaching rather than meetings and paperwork. Without the contribution of supply teachers, many institutions would be in even more desperate circumstances than they are already with the current recruitment and retention crises.

How many supply teachers are there?

Statistics show that in the last decade there has seen a significant, but rarely discussed, rise in the number of supply teachers. According to findings from the 9 November 2001 report by the Institute of Public Policy Research in London:

☐ The use of supply teachers is increasing, especially in those schools the government is most worried about, urban secondary schools

☐ The number of 'occasional teachers' (defined by the DfES as teachers working on contracts of one month or less) makes up a quarter of the much trumpeted 8,000 increase in teachers during the past year

☐ The number of supply teachers on long term contracts is rising, making it more difficult to find qualified supply teachers for short term cover

☐ Supply teaching is becoming a more popular choice for experienced teaching staff who move sectors to escape some of the burdens of a full-time permanent post

☐ A conservative estimate is that schools are spending £600m annually on supply teachers. This amounts to 3.4% of the entire expenditure of LEA maintained schools in England, and 5.3% of the entire expenditure on teachers. Schools are spending approximately twice as much on supply teachers as on computers.

(For more information contact the IPPR Press Office: 020 7470 6120/ 07932 749095 and Joe Hallgarten, IPPR education researcher: 07946 381576/020 7470 0024)

The report identifies several reasons for this shift. These include the flexibility, and for younger or non-UK trained teachers, the better pay supply teaching can offer. The increased demand has decreased the levels of job insecurity normally associated with temporary work. It also reflects the status of the profession; supply teachers are better protected against problems such as low autonomy and excessive workload, and may be more able to filter out their worst effects. As one supply teacher told me in a staff-room, 'I want to teach, but I don't want to be a teacher.'

Judging from the staff-rooms I have been in, it would appear that the main group (around 60%) of supply teachers are qualified teachers from outside of the UK. That pool of supply teachers is constantly changing as these teachers go home and more arrive on the shores of England. A recent recruitment drive in South Africa attracted 140 for the London borough of Tower Hamlets. Waltham Forest was getting 70 from Australia. Other authorities are targeting New Zealand and Canada. The other 40% of supply teachers are UK trained teachers where the pool is more consistent, being made up largely of teachers with other commitments or teachers who have taken an early retirement.

Availability and frequency of supply work

Supply teachers are a natural port of call in a crisis. Given all the news-paper reports of just how desperate the crisis is in recruitment and retention in the education system in England and Wales – though less so in Scotland and Northern Ireland – it would seem that you are in a good position to be offered frequent work as a supply teacher. Such reports are not based just on anecdotal accounts. Schools in England and Wales make frequent use of supply teachers. On average primary schools use supply teachers at least one day per week and secondary schools approximately four days per week. In the last financial year, schools spent an average of £43.00 per student from their budget on supply teachers. This breaks down to £50.78 for primary schools and £32.80 for secondary schools. The use of supply teachers is normally an additional incurred expense.

It is particularly difficult to state how much work to expect in any given geographical region of the country or any town, village or city because the demand for your services depends upon a number of variables, in-cluding age levels and subject areas taught, experience such as SEN, and time of year in which you are able to work. The demand for primary teachers is consistently high, while pre-school and childcare centres are less predictable, and the demand for secondary teachers may vary de-pending on your subject area. If you are 0-5 trained it is recommend that you gain some experience with 5-7 year olds. Even a couple of days of voluntary work will increase your chance of consistent work. That said, if you are a competent and diligent teacher then you should expect to re-ceive a plentiful supply of work at all levels of Key Stages 1-4. A-level (AS and A2) are not normally given cover with a supply teacher as it is beyond compulsory education and learners are at an age where adult supervision is not mandatory. For more specific details on seasonal demand in your geographical area and speciality of teaching it is advisable to check with your supply agency consultant, LEA or school at the time of your registration.

Remember this when you arrive at a school at 8:30 a.m. The school needs you more than you need any specific school, as the students need to be learning, but having you is an extra expense. Do your job and you will be respected by the headteacher and colleagues and probably be called back when the next crisis arrives – maybe the next day. On the other side of the coin, also remember that you will not be the first supply teacher ever seen at that school, so excuse the occasionally dismissive attitude from administrative staff, other teachers and children. If you are not given access to staff-room and the key information you need – where to make coffee, where the toilets are – ask. Remind yourself and the school, politely, that today's supply teacher can be tomorrow's permanent teacher.

Long term or short term assignments?

When the call comes offering you a supply teaching assignment it may not always be the wanted call. How long is a piece of string – would you accept a long term assignment offered at the 'wrong school' or a short term assignment offered at the 'right school' when you prefer the opposite?

On day-to-day or short term work it is in the best interest for the school, if possible, to notify the supply agency and hence the teacher as far in advance as possible of an assignment, but this does not always happen. Unforeseen reasons for absence, such as illness, mean that daily vacancies are often placed the night beforehand, early in the morning or sometimes up to the start of the first lesson. Occasionally a teacher will also go home sick during the day. Be prepared to leave home at a moment's notice if you have already informed your supply agency that you are available for work. The supply agency will contact the supply teacher matching the school's requirements and give details of the cover needed and directions to the school. Day-to-day teachers need resilience, flexibility and excellent map reading skills!

Supply teaching offers complete flexibility to work as much and often you choose, which can fit in with caring for a family, travel plans, or study. As time goes on you will find that you will narrow down to a few schools in your area and you and the children will not be totally alien when you are called in. General cover or short term supply needs a teacher to be jack-of-all-trades being able to handle six different subjects in one day at a secondary school or being able to handle the most challenging Year 1 class in their second week of school.

Maternity leave or perhaps a colleague's unexpected long term illness or resignation may prompt a headteacher to contact a supply agency with a long term supply teaching position in the middle of a year. The students need to be learning! Be prepared for the fact that supply assignments of one or even two terms require a teacher to step into some-one else's shoes and out again at a moment notice and can include GCSE coursework and final examination preparation. Consider if you wish to do such a job without being on a direct contract for a school and usually not getting the same benefits. Normally, however, supply agencies receive notice of these vacancies between May and September when a vacancy has not been filled. So a supply teacher will be required for the first term in the first instance, while the vacancy is re-advertised. In such cases, the headteacher will normally interview the supply teacher before offering the long term supply work. Teaching for a term in one school offers greater stability and more opportunity to be involved in school life. Many an offer of a permanent position has arisen from a term's assignment.

Permanent and newly qualified teacher positions

Headteachers are obligated as government employers to advertise a vacant post, though increasingly they are asking supply agencies to act as recruitment companies to help them find the right member of staff. The supply agency is asked by a school to advertise the post on behalf of the school and to recruit a supply teacher from its database of registered teachers. Through regular university visits across the United Kingdom and recruitment overseas, supply agencies build up a pool of newly qualified and experienced teachers looking for such permanent posts. Headteachers stipulate their requirements and suitable candidates are put forward by the supply agencies, which take an introductory fee. Following a successful interview, the school will take on the teacher direct. The advantage of such a system is that if either party would like a trial period, then an agreed time such as half a term's initial supply teaching is an option.

Government expectations of supply teachers

Headteachers often tell supply teachers and government that the increase in use of supply teachers in schools must not be at the expense of quality of education. It is vitally important that supply teachers integrate themselves into the schools by abiding by the school's standards, ethos, policies and expectations. This is easier said than done if you are at five different schools in five days, each with a different student composition and hence different policy and expectations. In general, however, as a supply teacher you will be expected to adhere to the norms required of any qualified teacher. You will need to:

☐ Keep up to date on National Curriculum issues and your subject speciality

☐ Telephone the school to establish required needs for advance bookings

☐ Teach and supervise classes effectively, as required by each particular school

☐ Prepare lessons, or teach ready-prepared lessons as appropriate

☐ Supply appropriate materials for emergency bookings in the primary sector

☐ Mark any written work by primary classes before leaving at the end of each day

☐ Mark work in secondary schools unless placement is for a single day

☐ Maintain professional standards of dress and behaviour

☐ Carry out reasonable requests made by the headteacher

The government's expectations state that you are a teacher in every sense but that you are not on contract to a school. This is the condition on which you are expected to teach. The school cannot request you for parents' evenings, for extra-curricular activities or for administrative duties. On the other hand, you do not receive a regular salary on the same scale, cannot receive London weighting allowance and only in rare circumstances will you be eligible for the same pension scheme. Sickness and holiday pay is a matter of contractual negotiation. This generates a special situation of advantages and disadvantages for both the school and for you.

Quality control of supply teachers

The Department for Education and Skills (DfES) has assured me that it is in the process of developing measures to adopt a positive policy towards supply teachers including: a quality mark scheme for agencies and LEAs supplying schools with temporary teachers; the production of self-study materials for supply teachers to keep their skills up to date; revised guidance for agencies and LEAs while new guidance is prepared to replace circular 7/96: *Use of Supply Teacher*, that will clarify responsibilities, set standards and give examples of good practice. To this purpose the consultation document, *Supply Teachers – Meeting the Challenge*, which was issued in early 2002 made a number of proposals to raise the status and quality of supply teaching. It would indeed be helpful to obtain a copy. Further, most headteachers I have met agree that supply teachers should be required to undertake some form of relevant professional development annually.

Nevertheless, the practicalities tend to elude the reality of what it takes to implement any framework of responsibilities for ensuring the closing of the gap between a teacher on contract to a school and a supply teacher working through a supply teacher agency or LEA. The allocation of funding is a major issue to train teachers working in several schools or for several agencies. Schools and agencies may not be willing to collaborate on cost sharing. Linked to this is the question of who should be responsible for monitoring and evaluating such training to ensure that the professional development needs of supply teachers are met.

Keeping up with curriculum changes and professional development.

The criticism often levelled against supply teachers, especially daily cover supply teachers, is that they are not keeping abreast of educational developments and are therefore not providing education at the same level as a teacher on contract to a school. It is a well-accepted fact that

UK trained teachers doing supply teaching do not have the luxury of in-service-educational-training (INSET) nor of paid-for professional development courses. Non-UK trained teachers doing supply teaching will initially not be familiar with the system of education or curriculum in the United Kingdom.

What skills and development would be needed should funding become available is a complex question. A distance-learning package would need to include practical sessions to enable teachers to discuss the training delivered by such packages. They would need to include: Information Communication Technology (ICT); Literacy and Numeracy strategies; Curriculum 2000; Behaviour Management; Planning; QTS standards; Science; Organisational arrangements; Health and Safety; Management Information; Planning; Child Protection; Code of Conduct; and Teaching styles.

To this end, the General Teaching Council (GTC) aims to provide advice and guidance towards professional development. It also works with all relevant government agencies and departments to explore the implications of curriculum change, for example in Key Stage 3, sixth form, and vocational GCSEs, for teachers' work and professional development. Some supply agencies also offer an afternoon seminar on certain issues such as classroom management. For more information consult GTC Teachers' Qualifications (see Contacts, p.119)

How you keep up with curriculum changes and professional development rests with you. Offers for supply work ultimately depend upon your performance in a school.

Keys skills needed to be a supply teacher

Before taking the plunge and becoming a supply teacher simply because you have time available and need some money, it would be prudent to consider some initial matters that rise from questions I have asked senior management teams (SMT). The information will help you know which priorities to emphasis as you set off early in the morning.

The key skills required of a primary school supply teacher as identified by SMT were:

☐ Good working knowledge of literacy and numeracy strategies (67%)

- ☐ Knowledge of the National Curriculum (44%)
- ☐ Effective behaviour management (44%)
- ☐ Classroom management techniques (40%)
- ☐ Understanding of or skills in Information Communication Technology (36%)
- ☐ Skills in assessment methods (22%)
- ☐ Knowledge and understanding of special education needs issues (15%)
- ☐ Knowledge of health and safety to be a requirement (4%)

Do you feel that perhaps all you need is a PGCE or equivalent? You would, with justification, feel that the answers reflect that the main requirements for a primary school supply teacher are to be a qualified teacher.

The key skills required of a secondary school supply teacher as identified by SMT were:

- ☐ Ability and knowledge to manage behaviour effectively (49%)
- ☐ Subject speciality in the curriculum area to be taught (43%)
- ☐ Classroom management techniques (42%)
- ☐ Knowledge of literacy and numeracy strategies (39%)
- ☐ Knowledge of the National Curriculum (36%)
- ☐ Understanding/skills in Information Communications Technology (33%)
- ☐ Skills in assessment methods (20%)
- ☐ Knowledge and understanding of special education needs (13%)
- ☐ Skills in inclusive education (6%)
- ☐ Knowledge of health and safety (4%)

Such responses reflect the worsening situation in schools, which have problems of recruitment and retention, and hence need supply teachers.

No doubt a PGCE or equivalent needs to be supplemented by an iron fist in a velvet glove and a strong sense of humour for you to survive and enjoy teaching in a secondary school.

What do others think of supply teachers?

Now you know the facts and the figures that will help you in your position as a supply teacher, what skills are most valued? In planning your future, being informed is being forewarned. Keep abreast of developments. Take note of opinions reported in the press. Take account of what they think of you.

After the Mayor of London met the Secretary of State for Education to discuss London's teacher shortage, he said:

> The rate of teacher vacancies in London is much higher than any-where else in England and has doubled between 1996 and 2000. Even so, I think the real figure far exceeds that, with headteachers papering over the cracks as best they can with short term contracts, supply staff, teachers from overseas and the appointment of in-appropriately qualified teachers. (News from the Mayor of London 5 March 2002 www.london.gov.uk/news/2002/112-0503.htm)

The General Secretary of the National Association of School Masters Union of Women Teachers (NASUWT) estimated the overall shortage of teachers was between 20,000 and 30,000. The gap was partly filled by supply teachers, mostly from abroad. In past years, teachers from Australia, New Zealand, South Africa and Canada provided temporary cover when permanent staff went sick. But now they were being used to fill long term vacancies. 'These overseas teachers are good kids, but they come and go. They are not the right way to staff schools per-manently because their turnover is too high.' (*The Guardian* 'Overseas staff plug the gaps' 21/3/2001 society.guardian.co.uk/commongood/comment/0,8146,460101,00.html)

2

Making the Jump

It may seem that you are now ready to make the jump. You want to teach and you want to be a supply teacher. You do not want to be a teacher in the traditional sense of going to the same school every day, teaching the same students every day, seeing the same colleagues every day and being obligated by a contract with the school in order to teach. You also want to have the option to return to being on contract with a school. You want to keep your hand in the profession and keep up with developments while broadening your experience. So the jump is not permanent. Your decision to become a supply teacher could be born out of having young children and wanting to work three instead of five days a week. Or you may be returning from sick leave. Alternatively as more and more teachers are offered short term contracts and the number of temporary jobs is increasing, you find yourself being forced to consider working as a supply teacher. Additionally you could be a visiting qualified teacher from another country on a restricted work-travel visa and thus eligible only for supply teaching.

Supply teaching can offer rich alternatives: you can teach every day but in a different school; you can teach children every day but different children; you can have colleagues in the staff-room and socialise after school but with different colleagues every day. Surely this is tiring, you may ask. Yes, it is. It is also stressful having a new environment every day so perhaps a new school every week or every month or every term might suit you better. There is more about the differences between daily versus long term supply later on in this book. No matter which option you chose supply teaching would provide you with as many or as few contractual obligations as you wish. That means you could be registered with one supply agency or ten, with one LEA or as many LEAs as there are within commuting distance. Best of all, you do not have to accept an assignment – maybe you are doing other things that day or maybe you have had bad experiences at a certain school and have no wish to go back. Supply teaching means that you are in control of when you work and to a certain extent where you work.

Whatever your particular circumstances, you should be aware that supply teaching is potentially more complicated than being a permanent staff member and sometimes the legal position of supply agency teachers is ambiguous. Recently in the news was an agency that hired FE lecturers based upon legal loopholes. Another agency was placed in charge of a government scheme but failed to inform government that the scheme was not properly regulated, thus permitting fraud. Yet another agency ignored warnings from a school that one of its teachers was at risk to be teaching children and this subsequently led to legal action after the teacher proved, at a different school, to be unsuitable – the agency not having followed proper investigative procedures. Take heed of the news and move to another agency should you feel that your reputation is being threatened!

How to become a supply teacher

Once you have made the decision or the decision has been made for you, what do you do next? What are the practicalities of becoming a supply teacher? Generally you have to be a qualified teacher before you can become a supply teacher for schools but there are certain exceptions. It is best to check with GTC Teachers' Qualifications Section (See Contacts, p.119). You do not have to have United Kingdom Qualified Teacher Status (QTS). You could be a Newly Qualified (NQT) UK trained teacher or a non-UK trained teacher. The various qualifications and options are explained below. This differs from North America for example where some states hire parents after they have done a short induction course. Supply teaching in the UK is intended to be teaching and not babysitting.

The sources of supply teachers for schools include: pools of supply teachers maintained by an LEA; the school's own external contacts; part-time teachers working at the institution or locally who are willing temporarily to work extra hours, and employment, business and supply teacher agencies. Sometimes it is not which agencies and Local Education Authorities are on offer to the supply teacher but also what these do for the supply teacher other than finding a job.

Qualified Teacher Status

To teach in a maintained school in England it is generally necessary to hold Qualified Teacher Status (QTS) and with effect from June 2001 to be registered with the General Teaching Council for England. QTS is normally obtained by undertaking a recognized course of initial teacher training (ITT) in England. So if you are a UK qualified teacher with qualified teacher status you are eligible to apply straight away for any potential supply position.

Non-UK trained teacher

You may however be a non-UK trained teacher. The criteria for your employment needs to be specifically checked and may vary from instance to instance. Current regulations do not allow for the automatic recognition of teaching qualifications gained abroad, unless the teacher is a national of a member state of the European Economic Area (EEA) and a trained qualified state school teacher in one of the following EEA member states: Austria, Belgium, Denmark, Finland, France, Germany, Greece, Iceland, Ireland, Italy, Liechtenstein, Luxembourg, Netherlands, Norway, Portugal, Spain, Sweden and the United Kingdom. This mutual recognition is the result of an agreement between those countries and is covered by EC Directive 89/48. Verification of these EEA qualifications can be sought through the GTC Teachers' Qualifications Section (See Contacts, p.119).

The Education (Teachers) Qualifications and Health Standards Regulations 1999 (SI 1999 No. 2166) (as amended) allow schools to appoint overseas-trained teachers without UK-QTS in three possible circumstances: as trainees on an employment-based route; as a temporary teacher in a school or a number of schools for up to four years without QTS (this is considered supply teaching); and as 'instructors' – persons offering particular skills who may be appointed when no qualified teacher with such skills is available. The latter is often the case in, for example, art, design and technology, food technology, music and physical education.

Advice on the level and standard of non-EEA overseas teaching qualifications can be obtained from the UK National Academic Recognition Information Centre (see Contacts, p.000).

Alternative routes to attaining teacher status to become a supply teacher

Supply teaching is not restricted to those who are either a UK trained teacher with QTS or an overseas trained teacher. In addition you may be a newly qualified teacher (NQT), either UK or non-UK trained. The range of training provision to become a newly qualified teacher is diverse and flexible. Undergraduate and postgraduate ITT programmes are available by full or part-time study, and some postgraduate programmes are available by distance learning. The undergraduate route combines degree studies with QTS. The course at a university or college will lead to a degree, usually BEd, BA or BSc, and to QTS. A full-time undergraduate course will usually last three or four years and combine subject and professional studies with practical teaching experience in schools. Applications for undergraduate courses are made through the Universities and College Admissions Service (UCAS). It is recommended that applications should be submitted by December, although some providers may be prepared to accept late applicants.

The postgraduate route generally leads to a university award of the Postgraduate Certificate in Education (PGCE), as well as QTS. This is the most popular route for secondary teaching, and is increasingly popular for primary teaching. To follow this route individuals need a degree (or equivalent) that gives the required foundation for the subject and age-range the individual wants to teach. Most postgraduate PGCE courses are for one full-time academic year. Applications to most postgraduate courses are made through the Graduate Teacher Training Registry (GTTR). It is recommended that applications to primary PGCE courses be submitted by December, although some providers may be prepared to accept late applicants. There is no deadline for application to secondary courses.

A small number of providers are offering new modular postgraduate study that allows trainees to follow more individualised programmes. Following an initial assessment of training needs, each candidate is given an individual training plan which takes account of personal circumstances and preferred mode and timing of training. The programme finishes with a consolidated period of teaching that is assessed. For candidates who have trained overseas there is the opportunity to take the final assessed period of teaching without further training. For further information contact the Teacher Training Agency (TTA) teaching information line Tel: 0845 6000 991. For advice about whether you would be eligible for student loans and/or help with tuition fees, contact the Student Support Helpline on 0800 731 9133, or visit the website www. dfes.gov.uk/studentsupport

The employment-based route is another form of training that may be particularly relevant to overseas trained teachers from outside the EEA. These routes allow overseas trained candidates to be assessed to obtain QTS relatively quickly where they have appropriate qualifications and experience. They provide training opportunities for people aged 24 and over for whom a traditional course of ITT may not be readily accessible. The Graduate Teacher Programme (GTP) enables candidates to work as teachers while following an approved training programme designed to enable them to attain QTS. It generally lasts for one year. For people who have trained and qualified overseas there is no minimum age requirement.

It is also possible for overseas trained teachers with at least two years teaching experience to be assessed against the Induction Standards while on the Graduate Teacher Programme. If the assessment is successful they will be exempt from the requirement to serve a statutory induction period after being awarded QTS. The first step for those interested in pursuing either route is to gain employment at a school willing to provide an opportunity to follow the programme. For information, see the TTA's website www.canteach.gov.uk or telephone 0118 952 3966.

Employment criteria for UK newly qualified teachers (NQTs)

After you have undergone teacher training you can apply to become a supply teacher, as you are classified as a newly qualified teacher. In general terms, teachers who obtain qualified teacher status after 7 May

1999 must successfully complete an induction period of three school terms (or equivalent) in order to remain eligible for employment as a teacher in maintained schools and non-maintained special schools. The LEAs are responsible for deciding whether the newly qualified teacher has met the Induction Standards on the basis of the headteacher's recommendation. Supply teachers working for less than one school term in any one post are also exempt from induction for one year plus one term from the date of their first supply post. The criterion for your continued employment as a supply teacher needs to be specifically checked and varies from instance to instance.

Employment checks

In all instances, UK trained with QTS, non-UK trained, or UK NQT, the supply teacher will need to undergo a vetting process on application to be a supply teacher. The first stage of this is pre-employment checks. You should be aware that the following checks are almost 100% likely to be undertaken before you are employed as a supply teacher.

- [ ] Identity: an employer may verify your identity by reference to a passport or birth certificate or any other valid photo-ID

- [ ] Permission to work in the United Kingdom

- [ ] Qualifications

- [ ] Health: you must be mentally and physically fit to be able to teach

- [ ] References: your prospective employer will wish to have references relating to your teaching skills and experience, most likely from your previous employer or teacher training institute

- [ ] Barred teachers: the employer or agency would be acting negligently if it failed to check to ensure that your name is not on List 99 (List 99 is the list retained by DfES of individuals who are subject to restrictions or barred from teaching and work involving regular contact with children or young persons in schools)

- [ ] Criminal Records: The Rehabilitation of Offenders Act 1974 does not apply to teachers and you should be aware that, if requested, you must give details of all criminal convictions (including cautions) and those that would normally be regarded as spent. You must ensure that the details you provide are correct and up to date. It is more than likely that the declaration you make will be checked against police records. This procedure is made through the Criminal Records Bureau, an executive agency of the Home Office.

With almost 100% certainty you will also be called for an interview where you will be required to bring originals of all documentation, most of which will be copied and held on file. At the interview you will have the chance to discuss wages and will sign a contract. You may wish to have legal advice before you sign the contract. Certain LEAs and supply agencies may also require a lesson observation. Certainly a school that wishes to have you on a regular basis will wish to see you in action, teaching in a class.

While your employer, such as a supply agency or LEA, should be in a position to provide the above information to a school, the ultimate responsibility rests with the school to ensure that the checks have been made and any further enquiries needed have been carried out. If your referees are slow to respond, this can delay your commencement of employment. On the other hand, it has been known for a teacher to register with a supply agency and start working the next morning. However long it takes, once you are past this administrative hurdle of pre-employment checks, you are considered eligible to be sent on an assignment to a school. From then on expect the phone to ring constantly, messages to be left on your answer-phone or voicemail, e-mail to flourish and text messages to wake you in the middle of the night. Your efforts as a supply teacher means that others profit: children's education; parents' happiness with a school; LEAs obligations to having a teacher in all classes met, and supply agencies' directors and shareholders who get a percentage of your wages.

Work permits for overseas trained teachers
One of the criteria for eligibility to teach as a supply teacher is to be legally entitled to work and reside in the United Kingdom. You can work if you are an EU national, hold dual nationality with the UK or an EU country – a dual second passport is required as proof. Patriality (British parent or grandparent) usually allows you to work in the UK for up to four years but may be subject to change; an EU born parent or grandparent may also give you eligibility to work in the UK and so may

spouses – marriage to a British or EU national entitles you to work in the UK, as does accompanying a spouse who has dual nationality, patriality or a work permit. If you are not a citizen of the European Union or a country with a reciprocal agreement such as Norway then you will need a work permit. No matter how severe the shortage of teachers, this law still applies.

In general terms the Immigration Service is responsible for deciding whether someone may enter the UK and what they are allowed to do here. People outside the UK who need advice on whether they need a work permit should contact the nearest British Embassy or High Commission. For people already in the UK the Home Office will advise. Some groups, including people born in Gibraltar and nationals of countries within the EEA, do not need permission to work in the UK and can be employed on the same basis as UK nationals. Some Commonwealth citizens may also work without a work permit if they had a grandparent born in the UK. Most other people will need permission to work here. If in doubt, prospective employers and teachers should seek advice from the Home Office, (see Contacts, p.119).

If the British Embassy abroad (or the Home Office in the UK) decides a person needs a work permit, the person's employer must apply to Work Permits (UK). The supply teacher cannot do this. Only the prospective employer, usually the school, can make applications for work permits. Teacher employment agencies are not eligible to apply for work permits. Agencies may, however, act in a representative capacity recruiting a teacher and submitting a work permit application on behalf of the employer. Work permits are only issued for specific temporary or permanent employment. In the case of teaching this means jobs requiring qualified and experienced graduate teachers. They are not issued for casual or *ad hoc* work as a day-to-day short term supply teacher. This differs from Commonwealth working holiday visas.

Work Permits (UK) is sympathetic to the difficulties schools are experiencing in recruiting teachers. Where a school can only fill a post by recruiting an overseas teacher a work permit application will normally be approved. Work Permits (UK) aims to decide 75 percent of applications within four weeks of receipt. For people who are already in the UK the final approval rests with the Home Office. Employers can use www. workpermits.gov.uk to download work permit application forms and comprehensive guidance notes. The guidance notes give a full explanation of the work permit criteria and details of how to apply, along with general information on who needs a work permit and useful addresses, e.g. the Home Office. Paper copies of forms and guidance notes can also be obtained (Tel: 01144 259 4074).

Commonwealth nationals who have been admitted to the UK as working-holidaymakers may take casual work incidental to their holiday without the need for a work permit. Working holidaymakers are expected only to take incidental work, not pursue a career. In practice, this means that they could work as a supply (temporary or 'fill in') teacher on a part-time basis for most of their holiday, or full-time for up to half of their holiday (for a maximum of one year). However, on expiry of their working holiday visa they will not be permitted to continue working in the UK without a full work permit.

Generally speaking, the immigration rules require that a person's status should be determined before or upon entry to the UK and that status should be valid for the whole of their stay. However, where a teacher from overseas who came to the UK as a working holidaymaker is offered a permanent appointment, the prospective employer (school or LEA) would need to submit a work permit application to Work Permits (UK). Work experience gained as a working holidaymaker is not normally taken into account when considering a work permit application and a teacher's familiarity with a particular school through experience as a working holidaymaker is not in itself sufficient reason to approve a work permit application. The employer would need to satisfy Work Permits (UK) that they have a clear need to employ the teacher, i.e. that they had advertised the post but had failed to recruit a suitable teacher from the resident workforce.

Employment options

The real question is who to approach to be a supply teacher once you have met the above-mentioned pre-employment criteria and checks. The best employment conditions available for supply teachers are for working in a pool maintained by an LEA or directly for a school. These conditions normally include:

- ☐ The right to be paid in accordance with and by reference to the school teachers' pay and conditions document

☐ The right to be a member of and make contributions towards the Teachers' Super-annuation Scheme (TSS)

☐ The right to a redundancy payment

☐ The right not to be unfairly dismissed (provided that you have two years of continuous years of employment with the same employer)

Working for a supply teachers agency on a contract for services will not normally give you these conditions. This is explained below.

Employment in England

A qualified teacher in England in maintained primary and secondary schools is generally employed via a direct contract with the schools themselves. Teaching vacancies are advertised in the national and local press as schools are government employers so are legally obliged to advertise vacancies. People seeking posts may also want to contact LEAs who may have some knowledge of vacancies likely to arise. A list of useful contacts, including sources of information on teaching vacancies, is available from the TTA's information line (Tel: 0845 6000 991). Those who wish to work in the London area may wish to check the website of Teachers for London www.teachers4london.com. The website contains information about London and a site to register details and search for suitable teaching posts. The TTA also operates a special help-line for teachers who have trained and qualified outside the UK (Tel: 0118 952 3966).

Contrary to the beliefs of the public, a school cannot simply call in a supply teacher when they feel like it, no matter how urgently it needs staff. Consequently, the first port of call for supply teachers is to take note of a school's advertisement and offer their services to the school directly or via the LEA should it be unable to fill the advertised vacancy. This approach is also useful for short term supply work. The LEA and school will then have your contact details and be aware of your availability should an emergency arise where they would need your services as a supply teacher.

Supply teaching in Wales and Northern Ireland

Devolution in Wales and Northern Ireland has given their national assemblies day-to-day and, to a certain extent, legislative control over education. Most national supply teaching agencies also cover Wales so obtaining supply teaching in Wales is much the same as in England. LEAs and schools in Wales follow the same practical processes as in England. There is a difference regarding supply teaching in Wales on the primary school level. Certain schools will tend to enforce local language instruction so long term supply may be problematic if you are not local. This is also the case in Ireland. Northern Ireland and the Republic of Ireland currently have a surplus of supply teachers so work is not readily available.

Supply teaching in Scotland

In Scotland the issue of supply teachers is an important part of the general issue of the overall recruitment and retention of teachers. There is no reliable information on supply/temporary teacher vacancies or costs in Scotland. According to the September 1998 Census, however, there were 2,919 supply teachers (with an FTE of 1,858, or 8 per cent of the total teaching force) in publicly funded primary schools. There were 2,370 supply teachers (with an FTE of 1,740, or 7 % of the total teaching force) in secondary schools. Just under half of these teachers in primary and just over half in secondary had been on a supply list for more than one year. Around 15% of supply teachers in primary and secondary schools had been on a supply list for more than five years.

From consultation with education authorities in Scotland, it appears that there are difficulties in maintaining an adequate pool of supply teachers in a range of subjects. Individual authorities operate different management methods for supply cover. Some authorities maintain central supply lists. In others cases schools make their own arrangements for short and medium term cover.

What does that mean for you? Education in Scotland has always been distinct from that in England and Wales. Scotland has a different examination system as well as a longer programme for both school and University. Scotland's compulsory education provision is for twelve years instead of the eleven years in England and Wales. Scotland also has a complex but fair examination system. Be prepared for the challenge. You may, however, have to look around further in Scotland than in England and Wales since there are not so many privately owned and commercially operated supply-teaching agencies. A good starting point would be to contact schools in the local area to ascertain the availability and frequency of supply teaching work.

Threshold payments for supply teachers

If a school or LEA employs you then you should know about the threshold. When the local education authority financial settlement was announced on 25 November 2001, the Secretary of State wrote to all authorities confirming that a special grant would be established to fund the pay uplift of all teachers passing the performance threshold. A particular issue arising from discussions with the national employers is the method of funding supply teachers who are eligible for threshold payments. This will be conducted retrospectively, based on two analysis points at the end of the academic year 2000/01 and the end of the grant period 31 March 2002. Headteachers have been advised that 'You should complete the SUPPLY3/4 to claim funding for those supply teachers who work at your school.'

If you are in doubt about your eligibility then talk to your employer, or ask your union. If you are not a union member, ask your local citizens' advice bureau. In general, supply teachers who have passed the threshold hold contracts with a school or LEA and are now paid on point 1 of the upper pay scale are eligible for payment. Supply teachers employed by agencies or self-employed are not eligible. All claims for supply teachers are made retrospectively. It will be for each LEA and the schools it maintains to establish the most efficient way of doing this. For example, some LEAs may make central arrangements for the threshold payment of pool/supply teachers. Heads should complete the funding claim forms for time worked at their school by eligible post-threshold supply teachers unless advised otherwise by their LEA. Supply teachers who have already passed the threshold should present their threshold letters of confirmation or a headed letter from the head of the school at which they were assessed as evidence of threshold status.

Where a supply teacher is assessed in 2002/03, the school may be notified of threshold status after the teacher has left the school, and should make a backdated payment to the teacher. If there is still doubt then fill in 'The supply teacher box' on the Threshold 2002/03 Assessments (TH3) form. This should be completed to obtain letters of confirmation for these teachers from the LEA. Headteachers should send completed letters of confirmation to the teachers. Supply teachers should use these letters of confirmation as evidence of threshold status.

Employment through a supply teacher agency

The three W questions apply to supply teacher agencies: why, what and where.

Why do supply teacher agencies exist? Schools and LEAs simply cannot find enough teachers. If advertisements for a full-time regular teacher go unanswered in the press, the school still has to find a teacher, or send the children home. Given that demand is greater than the supply of supply teachers it is not surprising that supply agencies proliferate. Working for a LEA or school may not give a supply teacher the wide range of options or the frequency of work desired. So a symbiosis exists for schools and supply teachers to consider each other's requirements to generate the best options for the children. Supply agencies provide the link. A supply teacher is normally self-employed and can therefore register with as many agencies as desired and a school is normally able to utilize as many supply teacher agencies as are needed and are available. First come – first served is the motto applying to supply teacher agencies.

What does it mean to work for a supply teacher agency? These agencies are normally Limited Liability Companies (Ltd) or sometimes a Publicly Listed Company (plc) on the stock exchange, that have been granted a license by the Department for Education and Skills. These agencies simply act as go-betweens to find a school a teacher and a teacher a school – on a daily or long term basis. Consequently the supply teacher is not normally eligible for the usual protections and benefits such as pension scheme, sick leave or threshold payments. Notwithstanding this, the supply teacher is considered a temporary worker and is still protected by certain basic legislation – such as the right to have a twenty minute paid break for every two hours work, and a lunch break in the middle of any working day.

The pre-employment vetting process applies and can take an afternoon or as long as your referees and qualification awarding authority requires. A school has the obligation to ensure that this vetting process has taken place before allowing you into a classroom. A supply agency can place you with a school on any type of arrangement that suits the school and you: half day, full day, week, month, term or even act as a recruitment agency for a direct contract with a school.

Contracts vary but in most cases you will remain self-employed. The position of teachers working for supply teacher agencies is less beneficial financially than working as a supply teacher for a LEA or for a school. There is no fixed rule, as each supply teacher agency will provide a different contract. Teachers working for some agencies will often have a contract that states that it is a 'contract for services' rather than a 'contract of service'. Such a contract might state:

- ☐ Supply Teachers are engaged under a contract for services which are set out below and apply to each and every assignment

- ☐ The Supply Agency agrees to offer the Supply teacher opportunities to work as a Supply Teacher where there are suitable assignments with a school

- ☐ The Supply Agency shall pay to the Supply Teacher remuneration calculated at a half-day or full day to be paid weekly in arrears. This is subject to the deductions for the purposes of National Insurance, PAYE or any other purpose the Supply Agency is required by law to make deductions. This relates to Earnings related Insurance and Income Tax under Schedule E, in accordance with the Finance Act (No.2) 1975 and transmitting these to Inland Revenue

- ☐ The Supply Teacher is not to engage in any activities detrimental to the Supply Agency

- ☐ The Supply Teacher and the Supply Agency agree that the nature of temporary work is such that there may be periods between assignments when no work is available

- ☐ The Supply Teacher is not to accept direct offers of work from a school where the agency made the introduction, without prior written permission from the Supply Agency. Doing so will render the teacher subject to charges in line with the Agency's loss of gross profit.

Some supply teacher agencies will deduct tax (Pay As You Earn – PAYE) and National Insurance (NI) contributions while noting on a pay-slip that Basic Gross Pay is inclusive of holiday pay. If a teacher can establish their status as an employee then they will become entitled to certain rights. CHECK WHEN YOU REGISTER – and if in doubt consult a citizen's advice bureau, a teachers' union or your own legal adviser. In all instances all teachers have statutory protections set out in equal opportunities legislation: any discrimination on the basis of race, sex, or disability will be unlawful. Discrimination on the basis of age is not unlawful.

Where are these supply teacher agencies? Some agencies are telesales call centres somewhere in the United Kingdom with a 0800 number and a www address, usually staffed by former teachers seeking greener pastures. They are called supply consultants and know the other side of the coin. Supply teaching employment agencies addresses can be found in their advertisements in the press. No one can hope to keep pace with the openings, closures, mergers and acquisitions of such agencies. Telephone Directory enquiries at 192 or www.bt.com or the Yellow Pages at 0800 600 900 or www.yell.co.uk will provide update contact points. As a starter, there is a listing of supply teacher agencies at the end of this book. The rationale for including these agencies and not others is that these agencies are members of the Recruitment and Employment Confederation that has a Code of Practice to set out clearly the responsibilities of employment businesses providing teachers and support staff to LEAs and schools in both the public and private sector.

Your own supply teacher agency

So none of these agencies suit you. The contractual terms do not seem favourable to your skills and experience. The consultants treat you like merchandise to be thrown from school to school each day. You get thirty-second phone calls from agencies and no respect from schools. So set up your own supply teacher agency. The difference between what agencies charges schools (£140-180 per day) and what agencies pay their teachers (£90-135 per day) means that despite the initial cost, it pays to run your own supply agency – even if you are the only person working for the company! As when forming any company, you need to buy an 'off the shelf' limited company of which you are sole or joint director (about £120). Register the company at Companies House – for details see their web site: Companies House www.companieshouse. gov.uk. Start work!

In order to start work you do what any other teacher or agency does. You find yourself a client or clients. These could be schools, LEAs or even subcontracting yourself to other supply agencies. Entrepreneurship is the name of the game. Undercut agencies, offer to mark homework, offer extra-mural revision for GCSE and A-levels. Being your own company means that the more you work the more you earn. Working for a school, LEA or agency means that no matter how hard you work you still get paid the same. Draw up a contract which could simply read 'I agree to teach for £X per day or per hour and you agree to pay me within seven days'. Teach and then invoice your client, usually on the spot before leaving the school.

Find yourself an accountant who will do your books or accounts for you at the end of each quarter, about £75 to £100 a quarter. This accountant will also be able to provide you with guidance about what deductions you can make for expenses and the minimum wage you set yourself. Pay yourself the weekly minimum wage to prevent incurring any tax. Remember that you must keep accurate records of where you worked each day. Also keep all receipts for travel, clothing and food, as you can claim certain expenses from your company. At the end of each quarter you can take a share of profits from your company. This will incur tax but it is usually much better than the tax on 'earnings'. Your accountant will be able to explain this process of paying wages, paying dividends or shares of the profit and how to make voluntary National Insurance contributions. Your nearest Inland Revenue (the UK tax office) will also be able to give you guidance.

Local Education Authority supply teacher agencies

If you can set up your own supply agency then so can they. Local Education Authorities (LEAs) are setting up their own teacher supply agencies to try to recruit more staff to fill vacancies and to reduce the money spent on private supply agencies. It would seem that the wheel has come a full circle. Twelve years ago the LEA handled most supply teaching requirements but then handed the task to privately owned and operated agencies. Now some LEAs wish for many reasons to take it back. Some are doing so more successfully than others.

The Wigan Council, for example, recently conducted an investigation and found that there was a huge demand for teacher supply cover in Wigan schools. Currently schools seek supply teachers through a mixture of private sector supply teacher agencies, the LEA's supply teacher list and individual contact with teachers known to particular schools. Difficulties with this system are well known and include the high cost of engaging teachers through agencies, the limited availability and poor quality of some supply teachers, time wasted in ringing numerous agencies to obtain cover, and the low rates of pay applied by some agencies. These issues have been discussed over the past year with a range of headteachers, teacher union representatives and colleagues from neighbouring North West authorities, a particularly active private supply teacher agency, Wigan Borough Partnership and senior Council officers. There is a consensus of support from officers, schools and unions for developing a broadly non-profit-making agency to be operated by Wigan Borough Partnership in conjunction with the LEA.

Similar processes of evaluation have been undertaken throughout the country. Nottingham City Council, for example, is establishing a scheme that promises teachers nationally agreed pay and conditions – and no commission charges off the money they earn. Its counterpart in North East Lincolnshire has set up a similar register called Nelstar, and now has some 280 teachers on its books. Similarly the Sheffield Education Services Supply Agency (SESSA) is a self-financing teacher supply agency established in 2001. The aim of the agency is to benefit all its schools and teachers. Over the previous two years schools had continually requested that the Education Directorate set up a Teacher Supply Agency. Brent Teacher Recruitment in Greater London services a supply pool for 98% of schools in Brent (four nursery schools, five special schools, 60 primary schools and thirteen secondary schools.)

So how does this form of supply teacher agency differ from other supply teacher agencies?

The main point of contention is that LEAs like to think that they do better than private supply agencies on issues of quality control. LEA-run supply agencies claim that some large nation-wide FTSE 100 recruitment agencies will promise both schools and supply teachers the sky in the marketed script and deliver a thunderstorm. LEAs supply agencies tend to recruit from the local area – teachers who had taken early retirement, or had been out of the profession and were looking to return. LEAs also note that they are paying teachers the national pay and conditions according to qualifications and experience, up to a maximum of the equivalent of point 9, and are not creaming off fees. They promise teachers annual pay rises in line with the national recommendations for England and Wales, eligibility for the teachers' pensions scheme, and the chance of ongoing training. If a school complained about a teacher it supplied and the complaint was justified, the teacher would be 'weeded out' and not sent to any other schools. Teacher unions are supporting such plans by Local Government Associations to set up a public sector supply agency to fill vacancies in schools and stop profiteering by some private companies. The downside response from teachers is that such agencies take too long to provide work and expect supply teachers to phone around themselves to look for assignments. LEAs also take too long to pass applications and many teachers feel they are inefficiently run – such as having no answer machine after hours.

The private supply agencies, however, doubt whether LEAs can compete with them. They claim that the teachers feel the advantage of working for a privately owned and commercially operated agency is that they offer more work and are paid more quickly than by LEAs, they take people aged over 65, and in some cases the work offered is more reliable. They think that if the LEAs had concentrated on retaining the teachers they already had they would not have the recruitment problems that permit private supply agencies to flourish. Private supply agencies claim that they make a profit out of efficiency, and that they have got massive economies of scale with gross profit margins in the industry in the region of 20%. They admit that the disadvantages include the fact that they pay no pension contributions, work could be cancelled at short notice, and some agencies were not interested in 'problem schools'. Agency teachers are also not permitted to apply to pass the threshold pay allowance and not all agencies offer training.

The good news is that *you* as a qualified teacher wishing to work as a supply teacher can work for all those seeking to employ supply teachers: schools, LEAs, LEA managed, operated or owned supply agencies, private supply agencies or your own supply agency. You can even register to work for all of these at the same time, though you will have to complete your own Inland Revenue Tax Returns, so keep all records of where and when you worked, how much gross you earned, and how much tax/PAYE and NI was deducted.

Dealing with a supply teacher agency consultant

Whether you work for an LEA, school, LEA-operated supply agency or a privately owned and commercially operated agency, you will have a point of call to contact for supply work.

Where former headteachers, LEA administrators or inspectors have set up supply agencies, supply agency consultants are generally former teachers. A cynic might label these supply agency consultants 'education telesales' and supply agency offices 'call-centres'. A realist would point out that the consultant is the person who calls the supply teacher in the morning offering the supply a position to teach. The consultant typically gets up earlier in the morning than the teacher. The early bird catches the worm and supply teaching is big business. The supply teacher may or may not accept the teaching position offered by the consultant. The consultant makes calls until all positions are filled. The consultant's job is not an easy one so be nice to the consultant and you will have a better chance of being given a supply position in a good school – even if you don't want or cannot accept it.

The consultant is a busy person, and has more supply positions to fill after the position offered to you is filled. Don't make the consultant wait for you to pick up the phone. Don't wait for the consultant to leave a voicemail. Sometimes the consultant will not wait and will not leave a message but will call another supply teacher instead.

Keep in mind that there is a person at the other end of the phone. That person is offering you a teaching position, and this is what you want. Your day will start off on the right foot if you are cheerful to this person. Say at once if you will not be able to teach. This makes the consultant happy. The consultant usually has a telephone recording machine or website set up for teachers planning on not being available to teach. Call in and leave a short message: leave your name, position/number and the days that you cannot make it to supply teach. This will also mean that you will not be woken at 7:00 a.m. by a ringing phone. The consultant is your friend. This person is providing an opportunity for you to work and make some money. Keep the consultant happy.

You are now armed with the information you need tp proceed.

3

The Nomadic Lifestyle:
your position as a supply teacher

Part of the nomadic lifestyle is deciding how frequently you wish to work – the choice is yours. There are some teachers who aim to work the full 189 teaching days as a career option. Other teachers, such as those with young children, prefer to work for shorter hours. Work is not always available when the supply teacher wants it. Exam periods, work experience and study leave, as in the third school term, reduce the need for supply teachers. Supply work may not always be available at the schools you want to teach in. This is not necessarily a reflection of the quality of the schools. You could prefer challenging schools at either end of the scale: top students demanding every second of your expertise or bottom students because of social problems outside of the school. It could also pertain to faith/denomination schools or single sex schools. Supply teaching is like any other commercial market. There is a supply curve and a demand curve and the production potential point of supply and demand moves on a daily and seasonal basis.

The purpose of this part of the survival guide is to provide you with an awareness that you will need to navigate this minefield of supply teaching successfully before you accept an assignment and afterwards, but before you enter the classroom. You will realize from the onset that your terms and conditions of employment and hence the expectations held of you will differ from those held of other teachers in the staff-room. Remember that insurance, tax and pensions are not a given. So before commencing employment as a supply teacher, whether as part of an LEA pool, at a particular school, or for an agency, establish clearly the terms and conditions of your employment.

If you work as a supply teacher in an LEA-maintained pool or at a school, you should ask whether your terms and conditions have been set out in writing – they should be. In the case of a supply teacher agency, the terms and conditions under which you will work are likely to be set out in a written contract to be made with the agency – sometimes supplemented by a handbook. Ensure that you understand the contents of any written documentation you receive and are asked to sign. If you are in doubt on any of the terms, seek clarification from the school, LEA or supply agency. If doubts persist contact your trade union, citizens advice bureau or a lawyer for guidance. Knowing what to ask is as important as the answers.

Being a supply teacher does not only entail knowing and adhering to a different set of laws and regulation pertaining to formalities of teaching as noted above. It also entails a different attitude towards life. You will need to adjust to nomadic classroom techniques, nomadic staff-room behaviour and accept the traits of a supply teacher.

Questions to ask before taking an assignment

For all supply teachers, key points to establish are:

What is the rate of pay for a full day or half day of supply work? If appropriate, what is the hourly rate?

Normally if you work with an agency this will be determined when you sign the contract to join the agency. Shop around. Join more than one agency. Some agencies offer bonus schemes. Ensure that your contract states when pay reviews will take place. Ask for a pay rise whenever you know you have done well at a school and they have asked you to return for another supply assignment. This is your strong moment to capitalise on your efforts and successes. If you are normally doing short term daily supply and then are offered long term supply, remember to ask for an appropriate increase in wages to reflect the increased workload.

What are your obligations when attending the school? Have they been spelt out clearly?

Don't tolerate schools that feel that they can exploit you since you are not a regular member of staff. Don't take it personally as this could and would happen to any supply teacher. Being asked on the spur of the moment to do a break duty is not picking on you and is not abuse even if you have just had a nightmare class. They are missing a person and you are just sitting in the staff-room.

Do you have insurance?

Insurance and liability taken out by schools, LEAs, supply teacher agencies and certain arrangements with trade unions with commercial insurance companies are aimed to cover you normally in the classroom, but what about the playground? Point this out and then say you would be happy to oblige for a break duty so long as the school takes responsibility. Break is over before it is settled. In most cases you are not actually covered for lunch duty as opposed to break duty. As a temporary worker, the school is obligated to give you twenty minutes paid break time for every two hours worked – quote the Department of Trade and Industry (DTI) Work Time Initiative (1998). Under the same law, lunch is unpaid and therefore you are not actually employed. This generates a loophole for insurance companies to state that you were uninsured, should some unforeseen incident happen involving you.

The insurance issue also applies for practical lessons in design and technology or woodwork or even food technology. If you are not qualified in these areas then Health and Safety regulations do not permit you to undertake practical lessons in these subjects. Make the school aware of this when you are given general cover. Better to lose a day's work than face an injured child, be injured yourself or face a tribunal for negligence.

Will you be required to do registration?

No harm in doing this. It normally takes ten minutes at the start of the day and then ten minutes after lunch or at the end of the day. Consider this time well spent, since you may be teaching the same children in a lesson and have therefore already introduced yourself and learnt a few names and faces. Black and red pens are needed for paper registration: red circle for absent and black diagonal for present. Black 'L' inside the red circle for Late. There are a wide range of other codes, should you know the reason for the child being absent, such as 'S' for sick. The school office will normally fill these in after they have contacted the child's home to ascertain his/her whereabouts. Make sure you also have a pencil for schools that use computer readable registration forms. Some schools will use BROMCOM or similar PDA computer registrations, which will be explained to you when you are given one. You can also use these for each class registration. They help to enforce your image of being a teacher and not a babysitter.

Is there a disciplinary procedure applicable to you?

In general, an oral warning is normally sufficient for badly behaved children. It puts them back in their places. At worst, ask the child to stand outside the classroom for five minutes. Be careful. Just say: 'stand outside for five minutes and then come back in.' Asking a child to leave and then forgetting about it could mean the end of your supply career. The child can walk off into the distance. A ten-minute detention is the maximum you can give. The law states that a detention longer than ten minutes has to be notified to parents/guardians no less than 24 hours before hand. Some schools also have a call-out system or corridor patrols. In such cases it is understood that incidents are the norm. Written referrals are common for the record, no matter what happened. Most children will calm down when they see you writing one.

As a supply teacher you have the same authority as a regular teacher and the same legal responsibility in the classroom. You are responsible for the safety of all the children, even from other children. *If a fight occurs between children in your class, what do you do? If a child is throwing objects such as pencils that might injure another child what do you do if they refuse to listen to you and stop? How do you restrain a violent child from damaging school property inside your classroom?*

Ask the school when you arrive in the morning for any specific procedures to be followed or if there are any known problematic children in the class you will cover. If no specific response is forthcoming then follow the law. The law is clear that you are not permitted to have physical contact with a child. But this generates an ambiguity. You feel the need to prevent violence but need to stay clear of it. In most cases the children will actually stop a fight or some will run into the corridor screaming 'FIGHT...FIGHT' and other teachers will come to help. At worst, if this does not happen, run next door for help.

Have the other children who were not involved write what they saw of the incident: the more documentation the better. Remember that the most damning request you can ask a headteacher is for the school's Disciplinary Policy Guidelines when you are writing an incident report. It means the school has a need for such Guidelines and that the incident which took place in front of you was not isolated and might well be run of the mill. Don't make a fuss about the incident with the headteacher. Headteachers are usually embarrassed when violent incidents take place in their schools. Calmly report what happened and hand over the documentation. Go make yourself a cup of tea and read the newspaper.

If you have a concern or grievance, are you able to raise it and, if so through what channel?

First port of call is the person in charge of supply. If this does not elicit a satisfactory response then take it further immediately. On short term supply (daily) and if you are working through the LEA or a supply agency, make the phone call as soon as possible, even from the school or off-site during break or lunch. If the situation is grave, call your trade union as well. Most unions have a legal help-line offering qualified legal assistance. Present a formidable wall as soon as possible. You are at school to teach and not to be aggrieved, whether by management, other teachers, children or support staff.

If you are unable to attend for work due to sickness, are there any provisions for sick pay (which is most likely to be statutory sick pay in any event)?

This will apply if you work for an agency run by a Local Education Authority, for the LEA or directly for a school. But it will not normally apply when you are working for a supply agency, as you are legally self-employed, even though the agency deducts PAYE Tax and NI. Check your contract before you sign it.

If you become pregnant is there an entitlement to maternity pay or maternity leave?

Check your contract before you sign it. Some contracts will explicitly exclude maternity pay or leave, though you can still rely on NHS procedures to obtain benefits if you are a European Union national or from a state that has reciprocal arrangements with the European Union. Some contracts make no mention of maternity so it will be a matter of inter-pretation, which is not desirable given the time that legal proceedings would take. As a rule of thumb, however, maternity pay or leave will not normally apply to a supply agency, as you are actually self-employed. It will normally apply if you work for an agency run by a Local Education Authority, for the LEA itself or directly for a school.

Who bears responsibility for making deductions for NI and tax pur-poses: is it to be you, the school, the LEA or the supply agency?

In many supply teacher agencies the responsibility for making these deductions rests with the agency but you may set up your own Limited Company, possibly 'off-shore', that will invoice the agency for your work. If in doubt, consult your local Inland Revenue advice office. The number is available from directory enquiries.

Who is responsible for the day-to-day supervision of your work? Has a line manager been identified to whom you can refer when you attend at the school, taking into account the level of your skills and experience?

The school has a person in charge of cover. This also includes cover undertaken by regular teachers and is not confined solely to cover undertaken by supply teachers. This person is normally your direct contact throughout the day, as classes may be re-housed in different rooms or the regular teacher may come back early from development training. Wait in the staff-room if you are not teaching so that you can be found easily.

What happens if you are unable to attend for work at a particular institution? Does the arrangement between you and the LEA school or supply agency come to an end? Are you obliged to accept an assignment offered to you? If you are ill, what steps do you have to take to advice, for example, the LEA, school or supply agency that you are not fit to attend work?

There is normally some flexibility. Everyone understands unforeseen circumstances. Your assignment as a supply teacher has most likely been created out of an unforeseen circumstance occurring with the teacher on contract. Call in to the person in charge or your supply agency as soon as you are aware that you cannot fill an assignment. The supply situation is critical so there is probably supply work once you return to work again. Never forget that you are a qualified teacher so can always apply for regular work or even move to another supply agency. Teachers are in demand.

Does the agency, school or LEA owe any obligation to you – for example, to find you suitable assignments?

Normally there is no obligation. The agency or even the LEA is a go-between and depends upon vacancies as and when they arise. No one can guarantee that a suitable assignment will be available for you on the day you wish to work. If you are flexible then you will be able to get more work, for example, being prepared to travel to a school on the other side of the city. Some agencies will offer a guaranteed payment scheme. This means that you have to work five days a week for whichever schools they assign you and in return if they are not able to find you work on any given day, you will receive 85% of your normal gross daily wage. Calculate the pros and cons of such a deal before you agree to it!

Obligations on accepting an assignment

Once you have accepted this assignment, what are the rules that apply to you when you take up your supply work? The starting point to your obligations is the recognition that you have accepted the teaching assignment offered. You now have a specific verbal agreement/contract. Your general obligations, which may vary according to the terms, set out in your overall written agreement/contract, whether the assignment is for one day or for an entire term are as follows:

- ☐ To arrive on time and leave the premises once the school day is finished

- ☐ To work the normal hours of work at the school (subject to any specific contractual arrangements to the contrary)

- ☐ To teach in accordance with the National Curriculum or to follow any lesson plan and cover work that might have been left for you

- ☐ To co-operate generally with other staff, and in particular to accept the supervision and reasonable instruction of an appropriate line manager, usually a head of department, assistant or deputy headteacher in secondary schools and the headteacher in primary schools.

- [ ] To observe the rules of the school; if you have any concerns (for example, about student discipline) you should identify these rules as quickly as possible by liasing with the your line manager

- [ ] To take reasonable steps to safeguard the health and safety of the children, yourself and other members of staff at the school

- [ ] If you have any concern about health and safety you should, with the assistance of the line manager referred to above, locate the health and safety policy and ensure that you comply with its contents

- [ ] Not to act in a manner that is detrimental to the school

- [ ] To keep confidential any information you acquire in your work relating to the school, LEA or supply agency.

Termination of a supply teaching assignment

Are there any notice provisions by reference to which the assignment may be brought to an end?

This will be set out in your contract of employment. Sometimes it just so happens that the school has advertised for the position that you are filling and someone has applied. The school by law has to advertise for vacancies. In some cases you might be eligible to apply for the vacancy. So if you have been assigned to a long term supply contract, ask the school the circumstances according to which your contract may be terminated. Remember that you are normally restricted to a defined length of supply teaching for any specific school and if you are a NQT or non-UK trained teacher you are also restricted in the sum total of supply teaching you can do as defined by the law. If you are working for a supply agency the school may be obliged to pay a finders fee to the supply agency should they wish to hire you as a full-time teacher on contract. This is particularly important for teachers engaged on a lengthy supply arrangement.

A school may terminate an assignment without notice and without giving any reason. You might simply be told that you are not needed back tomorrow. You have no recourse to challenge such a termination of assignment and it would be advisable not to challenge it. In most cases there is nothing wrong with what you are doing at the school – your assistance is simply no longer required. If there had been something wrong with your practice the school would seek a statement from you, as it is required by law to investigate and gather evidence.

Entry to the school premises

Are there any special instructions about gaining entry to the school premises?

Ask your supply agency or the LEA before you leave for the school. If they are in doubt, they can provide you with the school's telephone number. Most schools have tightened up security and only certain gates will be open. Some agencies or LEAs issue ID cards. Some agencies will send your details including a photo to the school. Some schools are on split sites or even on three sites. LEAs and agencies usually only have a postal address of one site for the purpose of sending an invoice. Sometimes these sites can be 20-30 minutes walk from each other, which would mean that you would be late if you go to the wrong site – Murphy's law says that no matter which site you go to it will always be the other site where you are needed. Never forget you are dealing with children and schools take children's personal security very seriously.

Returns on efforts – wages

Now that you have met all your obligations, you expect to be paid in return – a fair day's work for a fair day's wages. *So how do you ensure that you get paid for your work?*

When you sign your contract upon commencement of supply teaching, make sure that the employing authority or agency has advised you of the procedure to be followed to allow you to claim, and to ensure you receive, prompt payment. It is likely that any payment due to you will be conditional upon the submission of the appropriate paperwork and forms at the correct time. This normally means that you have completed a timesheet noting the hours/days that you have worked and that the person in charge at the school has signed it. Some timesheets also include a block to state that you have received your break times to comply with the Department of Trade and Industry (DTI) Work Time initiative (1998) for Temporary Workers.

Some agencies require you also to sign the timesheet. The timesheet will normally include such wording as to obligate the school to pay – that is to pay the supply agency. Normally a headteacher in a primary school or a deputy or assistant headteacher in a secondary school would sign this time sheet. In some cases the task has been delegated to the school bursar or other administrative officer. Remember that the employing authority/LEA or supply agency will not get their financial share of your efforts until this time-sheet is presented for payment. Neither will you. So it is in the interests of everyone to ensure that you fill it out correctly and have it signed by the right person. Most agencies or LEAs require you to submit the original timesheet to their offices, which you can do in person or by post. Keep a copy for your own records lest it get lost – it is the only proof that you have worked. Other agencies will let you fax the timesheet to their offices.

When will you get paid (perhaps weekly or monthly) and what about NI and tax?

Depending on your contractual agreement you will be paid weekly, fortnightly or monthly. In every case it will normally be in arrears. If it is weekly, you would need to ensure that the LEA or agency receives your signed timesheets by the Monday after the week you have worked in order to get paid that Friday. This will be stated in your contract. Remember that PAYE and NI are normally deducted under Schedule E no matter how many agencies you are registered with. This would not be the case, however, if you have declared yourself self-employed to Inland Revenue under Schedule D. Show this paperwork to the supply agency, LEA or school – whoever you are working for. You will then receive gross pay and be obliged to fill out your Inland Revenue forms yourself by way of Self Assessment and to make voluntary NI contributions. Maybe you are working for your Limited Liability Company that is subcontracting to the LEA or agency – paperwork and signatures still apply to get returns on your efforts.

Whatever your specific circumstance there are some commonalities. Ensure that you have the correct Tax Code from Inland Revenue. Each person's tax code will depend on his/her circumstances and will vary depending on such factors as age, marital status, child dependants, pensions, and professional subscriptions such as trade union membership. Enquire at your local Inland Revenue office about your own circumstances. Also ensure that you have provided either a P46 for first-time employees or a P45 from your last employment – this will ensure a continuity of tax code, tax/PAYE payments and NI contributions. Paying too much tax is not in your best interest and getting it reimbursed from an end of year P60 is not always easy, sometimes involving weeks of correspondence between your employers, Inland Revenue and yourself.

Tax issues for travel expenditure and other work-based claims

For the purposes of taxation, a supply teacher is not attached permanently to a particular school but performs relief duties at any school to which the employer directs him or her. The length of the spell of duty at a particular school varies between half a day and a school term (or longer). The school at which you are presently working is generally regarded as your permanent workplace so that payments made to you in travel between home and that school are emoluments chargeable under Section 19(1)1 ICTA 1988, are subject to PAYE. Expenses incurred by the teacher in travel to and from the school are not deductible under Section 198(1) ICTA 1988 because they are expenses of ordinary commuting. The main exception is where the frequency of changes in workplace and the nature of the duties are such that the employee can be said to hold a travelling appointment. If the travel and associated subsistence expenses would be allowable under Section 198(1) ICTA 1988, you can accept that their reimbursement (or scale equivalent) is not an assessable emolument. A similar situation applies with Inland Revenue for equipment used in the course of undertaking your job as a supply teacher.

If in doubt, deal with all issues of this nature by writing to your Inspector of Taxes or local Inland Revenue advice office. Before the Inspector can decide whether the travel, subsistence payments or other expenses should be taxed, he or she will need to know the exact nature of the employee's duties and the terms of the engagement.

How will you get paid – BACS or cheque?

The easiest and most efficient manner of getting paid is by BACS. You provide your employer with your bank details and they automatically transfer your wages into your bank account. So if you finish a week on a Friday and send the timesheet by post or fax to arrive no later than midday Monday of the following week, you will wake up on Friday morning with your wages in your account. If you are paid by cheque then you will have to wait for the post to arrive, make time to visit your bank and wait for the cheque to be cleared by the bank. This may take up to a week longer than being paid by the BACS system.

Keeping employment records

Teachers employed as supply teachers must keep careful records of the dates and schools at which they are employed and keep all timesheets and salary slips. This is not only for Inland Revenue, which requires you to keep your last five years of P60 (end of tax year) forms. These documents will also be needed for salary assessments particularly for the next annual increment should you go into full-time teaching on contract with a school. An experience point is awarded to a teacher (who does not already have the maximum number possible) on 1 September if s/he has been employed as a teacher for part of 26 weeks or more since the previous September, however small that part may be. It is also important that teachers keep these records and salary slips as they may also be needed many years later to investigate the amount of service for pension purposes. This applies to all teachers, agency teachers included, whatever type of contract they have. Self-employed teachers will also need to keep theirs for annual self-assessment of tax to Inland Revenue.

How much should you be paid?

How much you are paid depends on how well you negotiated with the LEA, school or supply agency when you signed your contract for services. The accepted starting point, if you have UK QTS status and have previously worked on a contract with a school and are now working as supply for a LEA or for schools is your correct point on the salary spine set out in the annually revised School Teacher's Pay and Conditions Document. It is calculated in the same way for all teachers. It is unusual, but not impossible, for supply teachers to be given points for anything other than qualifications and experience. If you are teaching wholly or mainly special education needs (SEN) statemented students, or in a special school, one mandatory special needs point must be added. Your supply teacher's salary may be calculated by reference to an hourly or daily rate, depending on the circumstances.

Three possible methods may be used for calculating the hourly rate: the annual salary according to the spine rate, divided by 195 (189 days of contact time and six days of INSET training) divided by the number of hours of the school day, in that school, lunch periods excluded but breaks included; or the annual salary divided by 1265 (the hours of directed time of a full-time teacher in a year); or the annual salary divided by 195, divided by 6%, multiplied by the number of hours of the normal school day in the school, lunch periods excluded. This is almost the same as 1265 / 195 = 6487 but appears to be different when set out thus and the resultant salary is slightly different.

The daily rate may be calculated in two ways: The annual salary divided by 195 (the days a teacher works in the year); or the annual salary divided by 1265 (the hours of directed time of a full-time teacher in a year), multiplied by the number of hours of the normal school day in that school, lunch periods excluded but breaks included.

Teachers working for supply agencies are not employees of the LEA or school and therefore are not entitled to receive rates of pay in accordance with the School Teacher's Pay and Conditions Document. Some supply agencies will follow the above method of pay calculations but without administrative scales, London weighting or recruitment and retention points. If you are a UK NQT or if you are a non-UK trained and qualified teacher, you should confirm the rate before starting work. Such rate normally varies from supply agency to supply agency, in different regions of the country, for short term or long term assignments. The worst case reported has been £65 for a full day and the best £147 for a full day.

Pensions and retirement

Supply teaching, like part-time teaching, does not automatically qualify for a pension scheme. In order to be pensionable it is necessary for a supply teacher working for a LEA or a school to elect to have super-annuation contributions deducted from his/her salary. The election form is contained inside the Teacher's Pension Guide to Part-Time teaching (Leaflet 476), which should be available from your employer.

Supply teachers working for a supply agency cannot normally pay super-annuation contributions even if they have elected to do so. This is because agencies are normally Ltd or plc companies that employ people under a contract for services. Under such circumstances it would be advisable to seek professional advice on planning for your retirement. This includes ascertaining your eligibility for a UK state pension since there is a set minimum number of years of NI contributions that are needed to receive a full state pension.

NOTE: Being in retirement and/or on a pension does not prevent you from continuing to teach. There are many supply teachers who return occasionally to their former schools or who are registered with supply agencies to lend a waged hand when the situation arises.

Restriction on future employment

Are there any provisions in the contract as a supply teacher that may restrict your employment in the future?

The best advice is to have your contract checked with your trade union, personal legal adviser or citizen's advice bureau before you sign it. Some agencies will include an introduction clause – that means they have contractually included potential restrictions on the employment of those who sign up/register with them. Restrictions could include schools, LEAs and teachers having to pay a finders fee to agencies if the teacher commences work on contract for a LEA or school after having previously worked for the school or LEA via the supply agency. Such restraints represent a major disincentive to schools and LEAs considering offering employment, and thus prevent teachers with whom they establish a successful working relationship, from taking up employment on a direct contract. However, there are doubts as to how far these restrictive covenants would be legally enforceable.

Your personal insurance, and various liability insurances

What is the insurance position, if for example, something goes wrong in the classroom, or if your personal belongings are stolen or damaged?

For the teacher: All sorts of things can happen in a classroom – mostly by accident or unintentionally though sometimes through mischief. It might be glue on the teacher's seat that ruins your best suit or dress, a leaky roof in the middle of winter which destroys your schemes of work, a mobile phone that cannot be found, your car being dented in the school car park by unknown causes, you slipping on a wet floor or even a physical fight where you inadvertently ends up being hit by both sides. Get your position on insurance clear and in writing before you start working. Supply agency consultants and LEA office staff may make promises over the phone but often do not know the exact details of each and every teacher. A teaching union can provide advice and in some cases offer insurance via a broker to cover every eventuality.

For the school: In general DfES Circular 7/96 (on the use of supply teachers) provides guidance on the different types of insurance an employer should have in place. In summary employers may be liable for the costs of injury sustained by their employees in the course of their employment. In practice, schools and LEAs have made arrangements for one or the other to take out such insurance especially to cover liability. Sometimes they have not and you the supply teacher would not know unless something happened. You are therefore advised to take out professional indemnity insurance (at your own expense) to cover potential claims for negligence. The trade unions can provide assistance and advice.

Registration with the General Teaching Council
All teachers working in maintained primary, special and secondary schools, non-maintained special schools and student referral units are required to register with the General Teaching Council for England, unless they are exempt from the requirement to hold Qualified Teacher Status (QTS). In effect, if you are in a teaching post that currently requires you to have QTS then you will be required to register. This includes part-time and supply teachers. Exemptions include: trainee teachers undertaking teaching practice; teachers working towards QTS through an employment-based programme; teachers trained overseas (outside the European Economic Area). Further information about the GTC and registration can be obtained from GTC Teachers' Qualifications (See Contacts, p.119).

WARNING – the worst case scenario of the nomadic lifestyle
We come now to the survival aspects in the classroom, the staff-room and, finally, the difficulties of being a nomadic lifestyle supply teacher. The starting point is to understand the process. The school has asked the LEA or supply agency consultant for a supply teacher, as the students need to be learning. You might only find out the realities of the job when you arrive at the school.

Normally the situation will be no different from any other first day at school as a teacher. The difference is that as a short term supply teacher you may have a first day as a teacher, every day, five days a week. There is always a group of students in the back of the room causing a commotion. You stop class and look at these students. Your glance is enough to stop them, but only temporarily. It's time to move a student – maybe because they have poor eyesight or hearing which is leading to boredom or maybe there is a social problem leading to in-class gangs. 'Please move here.'

You point to a seat in the front row. 'If there are any further infractions, you will be sent out.' While one child moves seats, the rest of the class is laughing and talking – you are no longer teaching them. Time for the heavy artillery: look down, pull out a detention slip and look at the class register. There is complete silence, accompanied by looks of surprise. The class now knows that they will have to deal with the headteacher should you refer any incident. The rest of the class is manageable, as are the other classes, as this sequence is repeated throughout the day. When the lesson ends and the students leave, your job continues until the room is at least as clean as when you entered, the work is marked if this is a primary school, and in all instances a report on the children and handover notes of work covered are written. This has been a typical day for the supply teacher. Some days are better than today, and some days are worse. So if everyone is getting what is wanted and needed, then who would think twice or even care? *Wrong*!

I was once told by my agency that a school would like me to fill in for a sick teacher. It could be till the end of the week, mid-term or the rest of the year. The school didn't know which, but they needed a teacher, so the students could be learning. It would be in my field of qualified speciality – Geography. The school would help me with setting up schemes of work. I would get a long term rate from the start (£10 extra per day). Would I like to take the position? asked my consultant on Monday afternoon in the second week of the third term. I knew that work would be sparse in the third term. Year 11 goes out early for GCSE exams. Year 10 goes on work experience. Year 9 sits SATS and supply teachers are not called in to invigilate examinations, which means that schools generally have extra in-house hands to fill the occasional sick days of their colleagues or hours that are used for curriculum development and training. So I agreed, thinking to myself it might just be till the end of the week anyway. *Stop!*

Ask your consultant for the school's contact and phone number. Call first before making a commitment. If this is not possible then agree to go only for one trial day to ascertain all the relevant details. Check exactly what your obligations will be. Ask for the EAL and SEN registrars. Meet the children. Talk to others in the staff-room especially other supply teachers. Find the librarian, who usually knows what's going on. If other teachers and senior management get apprehensive about you asking questions then you will know something is amiss. Then decide if you really want to take on the task, which may include preparing the students to get A-C grades for the Year 11 GCSE, take Year 7 on that 'forgot-to-mention' one day June trip to France, write end of year 'Third Term' progress reports for 350 children throughout Key Stage 3 and 4 in July – all of which makes you feel that a direct contract with the school might give you more value for your efforts than working through a supply agency. As you have not yet started work, the supply agency 'introduction fee' is not legally binding. Speak to the school. If they are really desperate for a teacher then they will agree to employ you directly on contract for the whole term.

Maybe all is OK but maybe not. Now you know, the librarian told you – she was a police officer but prefers working in a more stable environment. The teacher you are replacing is not really sick. In my case the teacher was a 26 year old who had financial problems with his houseshare, another teacher at the same school, and had not paid his bills for months, including car repayments. The credit agency and bailiffs were calling the school. The teacher had borrowed money from other teachers. Maybe this teacher had run away or maybe not. He was calling in at 7.00 a.m. and leaving a message on the school answer machine that he was sick. So the school was telling the truth but not the full story. The school needed a supply teacher for maybe four days, maybe till midterm or maybe till the end of the year. Do you still want the job under such circumstances, given that there probably plenty more day-to-day supply positions available through many agencies?

If the answer is Yes, that you still want this job on initial impressions then look at the children. You will be working with them. The children appear to be well behaved and motivated, the school has the resources and senior management are willing to be supportive. Take a few more steps and ask a few more questions before you accept, even if it is just till the end of the week. Maybe because the situation looks too good to be true – a walkover is never just that. Check the children's books. Ask to see the teacher's planner and marking record. Are you on a rescue mission or are you going to be the supply teacher that the school blames for the faults of your predecessor or even predecessors? Just how did such a good school with impressive senior management come to hire such a person as your predecessor? Maybe the school's attitude is that if everyone is getting what they want, then who would care? You get a third term job and your money, the school gets a teacher to keep the children in class and busy, and maybe all will work out and if not *you* are the scapegoat. So what are the options?

So why did I turn down that assignment – it looks like an adventure, which no doubt my predecessor thought too. In reality however the situation is the obverse of what normally happens. Replacing a bad egg of a regular teacher is rare. More often you are replacing a good teacher who has quit because he or she was not getting ahead in a school that was sliding for some reason. In most such cases the school is actually a sanctuary for children and staff escaping the outside realities. You are the interloper. Either you will become the outcast because you are unique in not being part of such social issues or else you will become entangled in trying to tackle them, even if only for a few of your students. Be professional and recognise why you are doing supply teaching and are not on a full-time contract for a school. Having a nomadic lifestyle means that you have to take extra precautions, ask more questions and think more about the situations that you are getting involved in.

The staff-room – your sanctuary, your office, your home away from home

Having a nomadic lifestyle means that the staff-room is where you will find your best friends and your worst enemies. The staff-room can be that rewarding place to make new acquaintances and socialise. Supply teaching can be a lonely job so the end of term or Christmas party should be opened up to you too. Take full advantage of such offers – they will help the school and you feel more at ease with each other on future assignments.

There is neither a right nor a wrong way to handle the staff-room. Playing it by ear is the best advice. The staff-room is also your office as you are normally expected to be at school about 30 minutes before the first lesson – around 8:30 a.m. It is here that you will meet your line manager and/or obtain cover work for the day given to you by another teacher or maybe just pinned onto the notice board. During breaks, maybe lunch and the possible free lesson, you will be required to be in the staff-room. Most supply agencies insist that you remain in the staff-room should the school need you during a free lesson, for example to cover a member of senior management called away from class on an emergency. The school is not happy about teachers playing the Internet in the computer lab or sunning themselves on the football field. Schools may have departmental offices with a kettle and a microwave. Check to see whether there is a staff association and if you need to pay for tea/ coffee. Others schools are lucky enough to be near High Streets for your lunch break. Ask permission before you leave the school premises.

Dos and don'ts in the staff-room

At the start of the day, look over your cover timetable and times, the cover sheet and work if provided, the class registers including EAL, EMAG and SEN, the school map including fire exits and the school's behaviour guidelines. Normally the head of department will also give you a few minutes prep talk. Though sometimes you will be covering for the Head of Department, in which case find someone else from that department if you can. Always look busy. Bring a book, magazine or newspaper to read in case of a free lesson. Bored supply teachers tend to antagonise other teachers fighting to keep their heads above water marking exam scripts and homework and writing progress reports. Don't ask teachers questions about the school. You might be shocked at what you learn from some teachers who are leaving soon. You don't want to inadvertently join a camp or be labelled.

It is also in the staff-room that you will meet other supply teachers, some from other supply agencies. Refrain from gossiping about other schools or the agencies. Such talk can get around and, gossip being what it is, the story will not end as it started. Talk about sport, art or the architecture of the schools and the neighbourhoods you have taught in as a supply teacher. Stay in your corner if you are unsure. If the school is paranoid about strangers you can be accused of eavesdropping for Ofsted, the LEA, the local newspaper or worse.

Traits of a supply teacher

The reasons for becoming a supply teacher will dictate whether the nomadic lifestyle will suit you or not. First and foremost however, you are a teacher and the students need to be learning. When I was in training to become a teacher, I encountered long and intimidating descriptions of all the qualities a person needed to be a teacher. However, all you really need is a love of the subject you have chosen to teach. That plus an overwhelming desire and ambition to make sure all the students in your classes master the subject you're teaching. This is a job. It is not your family and it is not your social life. This does not differ when you undertake supply teaching though as you go from school to school you may well find many new friends in the staff-room.

There is nothing more to it. If you really have a love of your subject and the goal of ensuring that your students master that subject, then your love of the subject will rub off on the students and you'll be able to acquire new skills and overcome any obstacles to achieve your goal. Whether you're naturally dominant or submissive, animated or quiet has nothing to do with it – your personality type is totally irrelevant. Everything you need to be a supply teacher can be acquired, learned and applied. Take a good look at admirable traits. Which ones have you mastered? On which do you fall short? What do you need to do to improve? Prioritise and take the next step for becoming more effective in a profession that depends on you.

Being nomadic is limited to the sum total of schools within commuting distance. In a small town or village this may be five to ten. In a large city this may be twenty. You don't get a second chance as a supply teacher. There is always another supply teacher behind you to take your place. Think carefully, act carefully, and be professional. Consider what you want to happen in the school and in the classroom. Never forget to ask the questions every day: what does a headteacher look for in a supply teacher, and what type of lifestyle do you want after school hours are over?

What makes a good supply teacher?

What makes a good teacher? At one time or another, most teachers who are serious about their teaching have probably asked themselves this question. The answers inevitably entail descriptions of particular characteristics or traits such as: interesting, knowledgeable, enthusiastic. Some might identify specific behaviours such as being able to explain difficult topics clearly and delivering well-organized classes. You don't want to be a sage on the stage – you want interactive learning. The children should be working as hard if not harder than you so be motivated and motivate the children.

If these are the answers to what makes you a good teacher then what is different when you ask: 'what makes a good supply teacher'? Firstly, as a supply teacher you might have a different school every day where you don't know the class, you don't know the children's names, and you don't know the regular teacher who you are filling in – could be 5 star or no star. A master list of additional qualities for a supply teacher would no doubt be headed by patience, flexibility, clear communication skills, and a sense of humour. Define flexibility in three ways: willingness to adjust to the needs of students; ability to change teaching based on what seems to work and doesn't work in the class; and being open-minded, tolerant and above all patient. Think of what it means for the children to have a different teacher each day and you will be better placed to understand how to be a better supply teacher. Place yourself in the children's shoes. The supply teacher most valued among students is making lessons that contain educational content fun.

The rule of thumb is to stop not regarding yourself as someone seeking to teach without being a real teacher and just cashing in for a day's work. Develop professional qualities that keep the students learning, wherever you work.

4

The Education System

So now you know, or think you know, what to do and that you want to do it – you want to be a supply teacher and you want to survive! Here's a short test, fellow supply teachers. Can you explain to me in detail: Beacon Schools, Education Action Zones, Excellence in Cities, Specialist Schools, Fresh Start Schools, Special Measure Schools and how to teach in each of them. Let me make it easier if you cannot. Define Key Stage 1 and 2 Literacy and Numeracy, and Key Stages 1, 2, 3 and 4 Homework, and Student Performance criteria and then give me the Schemes of Work showing study support, gender, ethnicity and achievement, parental involvement, and the use of resources. If you can answer all of this then please apply for the position of Secretary of State for Education – *your country needs you*!

Don't worry if you cannot, since your school needs you more than your country does. Headteachers constantly explain to government that they have problems keeping up since government have committees, sub-committees and working groups providing schools with volumes of information virtually daily. Nevertheless this chapter briefly explains what each of the above are, just in case it is relevant to the school you are assigned. More important, however, 'Have you kept up to date on National Curriculum issues and your subject speciality?' The supply teacher who knows the basics of the subject matter for each specific age group will be the supply teacher best equipped to face the specific needs of every school.

Terms, teaching days, INSET and holidays

There are 195 days in the school year of which 189 are contact days and the remaining six are set aside for training and professional development. The school year starts in September and ends the following July. The Department of Education and Skills has a website www.dfes.gov.uk with information on all aspects of the school system including a proposal to move from the three term year to a six term year. An approximate guide to the existing three-term year is as follows:

- ☐ Autumn Term: First week in September until third week in December. One-week half term break, usually the last week in October breaking the term into two groups of six weeks of teaching.

- ☐ Spring Term: First week of January until Easter. Easter varies each year and can be early or late in April. Normally there will be a one-week half-term break in the last week of February. So you may have seven weeks and then five weeks or five weeks and then seven weeks of teaching.

- ☐ Summer Term: This starts one/two weeks after Easter until third week in July. The one-week half term break normally falls in the last week of May to correspond with the late spring bank holiday. Depending on when Easter falls, you may have seven weeks and then six weeks teaching or four weeks and then six weeks.

The good news is that there are thirteen weeks holiday in total. The usual pattern is two weeks at Christmas, two weeks at Easter and six weeks in the summer, plus one week break in the middle of each of the three terms. If you are a non-UK trained teacher on a working holiday it is possible to work all available days and still have long holidays, providing you are on short term supply. Naturally, if you are on long term supply, you will find that you will do lesson preparation on weekends and in holidays before the start of the term. This is a grudge teachers have against the system – that an average working week could in some cases be well over 50 hours.

The six days of training or professional development are normally known as in-service educational training or INSET days. Schools will usually place these on the first or last day of a term, which adds to children's holiday and reduces stress levels on teachers. The first INSET of the year may well be lesson planning with the Head of Department. INSET during the year may well reflect an Ofsted inspection or the need to address the introduction of new resources, such as computers. Consequently short term supply teachers are not required for these days. If you are on long term supply for a school then ask if you wish to attend and confirm that you will be paid.

Nursery schools and childcare centres

Long-day childcare centres are known as day nurseries and can be privately owned or run by the local borough. They may or may not be attached to a school. The Children Act (1988) requires nurseries to be registered and at least half of the staff must have a two-year full-time qualification. Therefore Associate Diploma of Social Science (Childcare) and Diploma of Children studies (0-5) graduates can work in these settings. Pre-schools are also known as nurseries for 4 year olds, after which children enter the first year of formal learning in the reception class. Sometimes nursery nurses are employed as classroom assistants in both reception year and Year 1 and indeed throughout the school. The QCA have issued *Nursery Education – Desirable outcomes for children's learning on entering compulsory education* (2001), which is an outline based on developmental areas and is a useful guide for programming. Most nurseries and Montessori schools use this as their guideline for any programming, and inspections are also based on these criteria. In day nurseries the programme, particularly for the younger children, is based largely on the discretion and direction of the nursery manager. Many programmes are also based around themes and topics.

Supply teaching in these schools and centres is usually long term. This arises out of maternity leave or long term illness rather than vacancies that cannot be filled. It is unusual to take daily cover unless the Nursery school is attached to a primary school, where a supply teacher may be asked to go in for a few hours to lend a hand. This once happened to me. It was an experience to have fruit time, many sessions of supervised playtime intermingled with art and song time and then suddenly at midday, just as I was becoming accustomed to teaching at this level, the parents came to collect their children.

Primary and secondary schools

The United Kingdom has both public and private schools within all sectors of the education system. This means that some schools are run independent of state funding, some on a voluntary aided (VA) basis through a charity or foundation, and some with only state funding. This will not normally have an impact on your position as a supply teacher since you are not involved in the school's funding arrangements, though you will notice a difference in resources from school to school. Similarly there are schools that are classified as faith or denomination schools managed or operated under the auspices of religious bodies such as the Church of England (CE) or the Roman Catholic Church (RC). There are also schools that are state run where a single religious group predominate, simply because they serve a local area that has a mainly Muslim or Hindu population. There are no legal restraints to prevent you undertaking short or long term supply in any of these schools unless you feel uncomfortable because religious practices are a part of the daily activities.

UK trained teachers will be familiar with the sectors of education. For non-UK trained teachers the system is as follows: Primary schools teach 5-11 year olds. This constitutes Key Stage 1 and Key Stage 2 in England – each being three years. There have been significant changes in recent years to the way literacy and numeracy is taught in Primary Schools across England. In basic terms, an hour is dedicated to prescriptive activities for literacy and then a further hour for numeracy, usually every day. Although this may sound strangely dictatorial, it isn't. The teaching is well supported by resources and assessment tasks. In other words, you know exactly what needs to be achieved from each lesson taught and you are guided throughout.

The secondary sector caters for 11-18 year olds. The first three years are Key Stage 3 completed by end of Year 9 exams called SATs. The next two years are Key Stage 4. Examinations are taken at the age of Year 11, usually at ages 15-16 for the General Certificate of Secondary Education (GCSE). There are also General National Vocational Qualifications (GNVQ) Foundation and Intermediate Levels that can be taken instead of GCSE in certain subjects. This constitutes the end of compulsory education.

Since 1988, all state funded and most private schools in the UK conform to the teaching guidelines laid down by the National Curriculum. This is designed to raise teaching standards and give a consistent level of education across all schools. The core subject areas of the curriculum are English, Mathematics, Science, Design and Technology, Information and Communication Technology and Languages. Schools will also offer a selection of other subjects to provide a complete curriculum, such as Physical Education, Drama and Music.

After Key Stage 4, there is a wide range of options. One is for 16-18 year olds to be taught in sixth form or tertiary colleges that offer the Advanced Level (A Level). The A-level was studied full-time over two years but has now been broken down to one-year full-time study for advanced short (AS) level or two years for A2 level – the previous A-level. There is also General National Vocational Qualifications (GNVQ) Advanced Level that is the equivalent in study time of taking two A2 level courses. Entry into university is via a central clearing organization called UCAS that requires a combination of various AS or A2 or GNVQ at pre-determined standards of achievement.

For more details regarding the National Curriculum and what is taught within the subject areas it is recommended that you visit the Department of Education and Skills (DfES) web site www.dfes.gov.uk National Curriculum information is also available from major bookstores (e.g. W.H.Smith, Waterstones).

The range of schools
Knowing a school's classification, for example Beacon, faith, fresh start, or specialist school is just one part of being able to handle the system and the syllabus. Another is to understand the nature of gender and achievement within the education system and in society. In most LEAs you will still find heated debate over single sex versus mixed sex schools. Boys' underachievement is a major concern. Nationally, boys fall behind girls in early literacy skills and this gap in attainment widens with age. But that's not the whole story – many boys are doing well at school, while some girls are failing to reach their full potential. Underachievement may also be linked with other factors, such as local context, social class or ethnicity. Because tackling underachievement is such a complex issue and no two schools are the same, each school

tends to develop its own strategies, taking into account the character of the local community and the unique blend of its students. There is no harm in asking when you arrive at a school if the school is taking any specific notice and/or action of such issues and whether there is anything specific that you should do.

Bilingual children

This term describes children who speak a language other than English as their first language and are also learning via the Anglophone curriculum. So the term does not indicate the child's competence in any language. Teachers' attitudes to bilingual children are changing as they recognise bilingualism as an asset, which gives children access to two (or more) systems of thought. Many children whose families originate from the Indian sub-continent are likely to operate in several languages as are many refugee children e.g. from Afghanistan. A child's fluency in English, therefore, should not be seen as an indicator of general learning ability. Find out whether there is special EAL provision (English as an Additional Language) in the school and whether the EAL teacher, now funded under Ethnic Minority Achievement Grant (EMAG), expects to work with you as class teacher in lesson planning. The topic of ethnicity and achievement is well researched and documented but you should seek also guidance from the school management on the school's policy on Race Equality, as required by the Race Relations (Amendment) Act 2000.

Special educational needs schools (SEN)

There is no such thing as an average child, even in a system that prescribes a National Curriculum with textbooks endorsed by examination boards. Some children have specific learning needs that are addressed within the education system but separately from the mainstream. In addition to the SEN departments that are a feature of mainstream schools, there are SEN schools that provide an education for students at both primary and secondary age. SEN schools tend to have much smaller classes and children will usually be supported by a classroom assistant in addition to the teacher in secondary schools, or a Nursery Nurse in the primary schools.

The main types of SEN schools are for children with Emotional and Behavioural Difficulties (EBD), Moderate Learning Difficulties (MLD) and, Severe Learning Difficulties (SLD). Working with children with Special Educational Needs can be rewarding and interesting, but it takes a special type of teacher. Flexibility, empathy and patience, together with the ability to prepare and deliver individual and exciting teaching programmes are key to working in the SEN sector. It is inadvisable to offer to undertake supply teaching in such schools, even if only a daily basis, unless you are fully qualified for SEN teaching.

Beacon schools

As a long term supply teacher you should know what your role is in a Beacon School. You will certainly be expected to maintain a high standard of professionalism and teacher acumen. As a short term supply you should know you are in a challenging environment – the children will demand content and analysis rather than discipline.

All Beacon schools should be high-performing schools, providing a high quality education and delivering high standards for all their students. Schools do not refer themselves to the DfES but are short-listed by the DfES as eligible to apply on the basis of appearance in the most recent annual report of Her Majesty's Chief Inspector of Schools as a 'high performing' school or showing consistently high performance over a period of three to four years in relation to their school circumstances. In addition, LEAs can be asked to nominate schools that they consider suitable for Beacon status. Starting with a pilot group of 75 Beacon schools in September 1998, subsequent expansions have seen the network grow rapidly in the space of three years. By September 2001, there were 1000 Beacon schools in England and the numbers are growing. Beacon activities should be an integral part of the school development plan.

Education Action Zones (EAZ)

Short term supply teachers will not normally know the difference or feel any difference between a school that is in an Education Action Zone and a school that is not. long term supply teachers will be expected to contribute to that school's individual activities that may be to raise standards generally to initiate new activities.

Education Action Zones were an important part of the 1997 Labour Party manifesto for that year's general elections. Work on introducing these education action zones began as soon as the new Labour government took office. They take as a starting point two principles: that in the country's most deprived urban and rural areas, more needs to be done to ensure all students have the chance to succeed; and that it is essential that the school system has built into it the capacity for change and innovation. Education action zones are therefore about improvement and embedding change in particular areas, and also about discovering models of improvement that can be shared with the rest of the education system.

Zones were set up in response to applications from groups of schools and their partners. Applicants set out how they would raise standards, and set themselves demanding targets for improvement. Their plans had to be for new activities: it cannot be more of the same. Each zone receives up to £1 million each year, £500k from the DfES as a baseline and up to £500k more in return for funds raised from private partners. This is part of the government's Third Way philosophy of Public Private Partnerships (PPP).

There are currently 73 statutory EAZs across England and 102 EiC Action Zones – 25 'Round 1' zones started between September 1998 and January 1999, 48 'Round 2' zones started between September 1999 and June 2000, and 26 small zones started by September 2000 as part of the Excellence in Cities initiative. Large EAZs typically cover around 15-25 schools; i.e. two or three secondary schools and a small group of neighbouring primary and special schools. In small EAZs, there is generally only one secondary school; again this is linked with a cluster of local primary and special schools. Across the entire EAZ programme there are now around 1,500 zone schools.

Each zone is run by an Action Forum, and managed by a project director, a kind of chief executive for the zone. To help them innovate, zones have certain legislative freedoms: governing bodies can disapply the teachers' pay and conditions document so that new contracts can be set; and can cede powers to the forum. They can take advantage of existing flexibility in the curriculum, and of the legislation, which allows schools to disapply it if they can show that this will raise standards.

Excellence in Cities (EiC)

The Excellence in Cities scheme is an action plan intended to forge a step-change in tackling the particular educational problems faced by students in the major cities. It is mainly designed to address the under-representation of students from disadvantaged backgrounds in post-16 and Higher Education, and builds on the success of the EiC programme in secondary schools to improve links between universities, colleges and schools.

Both short term and long term supply teachers will probably notice the difference. Make sure that you know the status of the school before you arrive so you are prepared. Ask when you arrive at the school, to clarify the school's expectation of you. The general facts of the scheme are as follows:

☐ One of the key elements of the Excellence in Cities programme is the establishment of a network of school-based City Learning Centres (CLCs). It is planned to 100 CLCs operating in EiC areas across the country by March 2004. These will provide state-of-the art ICT-based learning opportunities for the students at the host school, for students at a network of surrounding schools and for the wider community. As a supply teacher you can expect to find plenty of computer workstations with high-speed Internet access and networked CD-ROMS. Take full advantage of the resources and facilities.

☐ The Specialist Schools scheme has been designed to promote improvement and diversity, with an emphasis on revitalising education. As a UK QTS trained supply teacher you can provide such diversity based upon your growing knowledge of many schools and different approaches. As a non-UK trained teacher you will be able to bring such diversity, given your knowledge of educational practices in other countries.

☐ The University of Warwick in partnership with the DfES will run the new Academy for Gifted and Talented (GT) Youth. It is expected to develop, implement, promote and support educational opportunities for gifted and talented children and young people aged up to 19, as well as providing support for parents and educators. Its range of services will include residential summer schools, online distance learning material and mentoring, outreach activities and research, evaluation and professional development. In the interim it is advisable to ask the person in charge of supply teachers at 08:30 a.m. if you have any GT children in the class. GT children can be very helpful in assisting. Make sure that they don't get bored or else you might be dealing with Einstein in the science lab seeking to prove that nuclear explosions do create mushroom clouds. Set extra, motivating and demanding work.

☐ The EiC scheme aims to increase the number of Learning Mentors in schools. These are school-based employees who, together with teaching and pastoral staff, assess, identify and work with the students who need extra help to overcome barriers to learning inside and outside school. They take some of the burden off teachers, who often feel as though they should be helping students to overcome problems inside and outside school. Having a learning mentor to help students tackle their problems frees teachers to teach. Check in the morning when you arrive at a school and co-ordinate with the learning mentor so both the school and you are able to make the most of your time – even if you are only at the school for one day.

☐ School-based Learning Support Units are an integral part of the EiC Scheme. These are for students at risk of exclusion and provide separate short term teaching and support programmes tailored to the needs of difficult students. They aim to keep students in school and working whilst their behaviour problems are tackled, helping to re-integrate them into mainstream classes as quickly as possible. The self-contained Units are small, taking between six and ten students at any one time and have a high staff to student ratio. Most Units take students from the school in which they are based, although a few provide for students from several schools. Most students attend the Units on a part-time basis to meet specific needs but a few with greater needs attend full-time. Get a class registrar for each class you are going to teach as soon as you arrive in school. This will identify who should be your class. Make sure that you don't have any extra children. Occasionally some children who are normally in such units will 'take time off' if they know a supply is in the school to enter your class and create havoc. Don't get angry; simply send another student to fetch someone to take the 'extra' out of your class.

☐ The Excellence in the Cities scheme includes Beacon Schools. Clusters are designed to bring the benefits of the Excellence in

Cities programme to smaller pockets of deprivation. Like Excellence in Cities, they focus on some of the most deprived areas of the country, using a structured programme designed to raise standards. Clusters benefit from extra resources to provide the three core strands of the Excellence in Cities programme: extended opportunities for gifted and talented students; access to full time learning mentors for students who need them in schools in the EiC areas; and Learning Support Units to tackle disruption.

☐ The Education Actions Zones (EAZ) as discussed before also form part of this scheme and many are now incorporated into EiC.

Specialist schools and colleges

One legacy of the ongoing evolution in the education system is the eight different types of specialist schools or colleges. These offer the four established specialities of Technology, Language, Sport, and Arts and the four new specialities of Business and Enterprise, Engineering, Science and Mathematics and Computing. Speciality generally influences funding and hence a percentage of intake criteria is fixed for children excelling in these areas. Supply teachers will notice the generous resources and also the children's aptitudes in the class. Expect to meet children who are more knowledgeable and more adept at undertaking specialist tasks than you are. These specialist schools are still obliged to teach the compulsory core subjects and here you will still probably encounter weak areas where you will be challenged to provide education. I can recollect one Picasso – a West African girl in the Art class in period one who sat very quietly and made some impressive charcoal portraits of her peers. In period three covering the same group for English, I discovered that she had only arrived in the United Kingdom two weeks earlier and that her English was still rudimentary.

Other situations

There are schools that are:

☐ Facing challenging circumstances

☐ In special measures, and

☐ Fresh start schools

A school may be classified by the LEA as facing challenging circumstances for a wide range of reasons. These might include serious financial problems in a given year, serious staff shortages, serious social problems on a short or long term basis dependent upon the neighbourhood, serious composition percentage imbalances such as the sudden arrival of refugee children or a combination of refugee children from conflicting groups. Such schools cannot be expected to have their results bench-marked against the national average. Consequently they often face difficulties in recruitment and retention of teachers. Supply teachers are often needed. Such schools also require extra provision for social workers, English as an additional language (EAL) teachers and Ethnic Minority Achievement Group (EMAG) support staff. One large three-site secondary school in central London, for example, had at one stage 62 different languages classified as the first language of its children. Supply teachers can face extremely bright and well-educated children in all such schools but motivation and communication issues might result in frustration. Talk to the headteacher first thing in the morning to make clear exactly what is expected of you in relation to the circumstances of the school.

A school generally enters special measures following an Ofsted inspection where Ofsted has found that management is not taking appropriate steps to resolve a difficult situation. The school is given a time limit in which to resolve them and more funding to assist. The Senior Management Team (SMT) and teachers who are sticking it out are pressurised to improve the examination results. Other staff might already have obtained jobs elsewhere. Such a mix is often dangerous. As a supply teacher you will feel immense pressure as well as apathy in these schools. Know your place as a supply teacher. Do NOT criticise a class of difficult children when you go to the staff-room at break or lunch. Regular teachers might feel that you are criticising the school. Offer your experience of diversity through actions in the classroom rather than words in the staff-room. Teach and you will be respected.

A school in special measures is closed if it is unable to attain better results in examinations over a prolonged period. The school is given a Fresh Start when it is closed and reopened – usually under a new name – on the same site under the normal school reorganisation procedures of a new senior management and the majority if not all the teachers.

Schools eligible for Fresh Start must be in special measures, have serious weaknesses, be subject to a formal LEA warning or (for secondary) achieving less than a 15% rate of students gaining at least five A*-C GCSEs. Ministers have made clear that Fresh Start should be reserved for cases where all other options, including closure or reorganisation, are impracticable. All Fresh Start proposals have to be approved at Ministerial level of government. On approval of any Fresh Start proposals, revenue and capital expenditure can be made available to support their implementation through the Fresh Start support programme. I once worked for six weeks in such a school. Everyone was motivated, since the Fresh Start programme included building a new library and sports facilities that would also serve as a community centre. It was challenging and indeed rewarding to see education happening before one's eyes every day in a school that had been struggling but was now succeeding.

It would be worth looking at Ofsted reports before you go to a school. Easier said than done, especially if you are only doing a single day's supply cover. If you have Internet access search www.oftsed.gov.uk and type the school's name. You will get the Ofsted report and the schools' website if it has one. Your supply agency, LEA or the school will also be able to fill you in on most of the details of challenging aspects if the school if you ask.

Office for Standards in Education (Ofsted)

A final point on the checklist of the education system is that of Ofsted's relationship with supply teachers. The Code of Practice, which requires inspectors to report confidentially to the headteacher on examples of particularly good or bad teaching they have observed, applies to all teachers in the school at the time of inspection – including supply teachers. Ofsted inspectors are expected to visit classes taught by supply teachers and the criteria applied for evaluation are the same as for classes taught by other teachers. A school will normally get six weeks warning before an Ofsted inspection. The aim of the inspection is for the school to self rectify any problems it considers that might exist. Generally a day-to-day supply teacher will thus not be involved in preparation though a long term supply teacher will receive the same preparatory INSET as regular teachers. Your Head of Department will help you to prepare. Generally you should have a scheme of work for the term and for that specific week, with lesson plans and class registers including EAL, SEN, and gifted and talented students. Children's work is expected to be on display in the school. Other than that just teach as normal, remembering not to lecture to the inspector – current practice is for a teacher to teach 20% of a lesson and the students to work for 80%. You are a teacher of children and are expected to prove not your knowledge but rather the ability of your students to gain knowledge themselves.

5

The Syllabus

Given that qualifications vary, the law is somewhat grey in the matters of which school you can teach in as a supply teacher. A UK earned Post-graduate Certificate in Education (PGCE) comes in three variations: Primary, Secondary and Further Education. Doing supply teaching in a school on a level other than the one you are trained in will feel as if you have never been trained. The law permits you to do so, and some supply agencies even offer an afternoon training seminar for conversion. There are also professional development conversion courses – check with the Teacher Training Agency (TTA). Non-UK trained teachers will feel even more alien when they enter any school at any level. A teacher with a BEd from France or a US K-12 will not even be familiar, for example, with the History taught in Year 7: Medieval History.

What you will need that Monday when you arrive at School X at 9.00 a.m. is to have spent the previous few days broadening your horizons. Get hold of the exemplar schemes of work from www.nc.uk.net – the government's definitive curriculum website for teachers. This site links every National Curriculum programme of study requirement to high-quality, relevant teaching resources and helps you understand that you are first and foremost a teacher. It is also possible to get the entire National Curriculum in hard print. Schools will have copies as will LEAs. Tell your supply agency which levels you feel competent in working. If you are only one step ahead of the children in content you are still in a position to be teaching them, because of your teaching skills and analytical abilities. If you are long term supply check with your school and they will advice you which examination board they use so you can get your own copy. As time goes on you will also find it prudent to read textbooks in the subjects you teach. The examination boards endorse certain textbooks and these should be your first but not final port of call. Often these exam board endorsed textbooks are the minimum need as a crutch for scholastically weak children and teachers who need a prop to remind them of the National Curriculum. A single textbook, for example, cannot cover the whole history syllabus, and indeed students need access to a broad range of texts and other resources to develop research skills. Your school learning resource centre or library will help with this.

The National Curriculum

The National Curriculum applies to students of compulsory school age in community and foundation schools, including community special schools and foundation special schools, and voluntary-aided and voluntary-controlled schools. For each key stage and for each subject, the National Curriculum is made up of two areas: programmes of study (which set out what students should be taught), attainment targets and level descriptions (which set out the expected standards of students' performance). It is for schools to choose how they organise their school curriculum to include the programmes of study. The curriculum is organised on the basis of four key stages, as opposite.

The Government believes that two hours of physical activity a week, that delivers the National Curriculum for physical education and extra-curricular activities, should be an aspiration for all schools. This applies throughout all key stages. Competitive games activities are compulsory throughout Key Stages 1 to 3. At Key Stage 4, although students can choose other activities instead of competitive team and individual games, schools should continue to provide these for students who wish to take up this option.

Exceptions to the National Curriculum

Schools have some discretion over when to start teaching the key stage programme of study. The law requires that they should be taught during

	Key stage 1	Key stage 2	Key stage 3	Key stage 4	
Age	5–7	7–11	11–14	14–16	
Year groups	1–2	3–6	7–9	10–11	
English	■	■	■	■	National Curriculum core subjects
Mathematics	■	■	■	●	
Science	■	■	■	●	
Design and technology	■	■	■	●	
Information and communication technology	■	■	■	■	
History	■	■	■		National Curriculum non-core foundation subjects
Geography	■	■	■		
Modern foreign languages			■	●	
Art and design	■	■	■		
Music	■	■	■		
Physical education	■	■	■	●	
Citizenship			►	►	

■ Statutory from August 2000
● Statutory from August 2001
► Statutory from August 2002

the key stage, not that they be introduced at a particular time or in any given lesson or period. The National Curriculum is thus a framework not a compulsory lesson-by-lesson obligation. As a short term supply teacher on a one day assignment there will be instances when you find that you cannot teach a particular class a particular subject, for example modern foreign languages if you are not a modern foreign language teacher and if no cover work has been set. This can occur in a school which, for example, has only one French teacher who fell sick that morning. So what do you do? There are two ways of approaching this – ask the Headteacher or person in charge of cover first. You could just have the children continue what they had been doing the previous lesson or give them a double-spread of a textbook. But then you are not teaching, just babysitting.

Alternatively, with permission, you could teach your subject area, so giving that class an extra period of study that week. The law permits this: The Education Act (1996) Chapter 56, Establishment of the National Curriculum by order 356 (3). An order made under subsection

(2) may not require: (a) the allocation of any particular period or periods of time during any key stage to the teaching of any programme of study or any matter, skill or process forming part of it; or (b) the making in school timetables of provision of any particular kind for the periods to be allocated to such teaching during any such stage.

It is possible thus to generate an inter-disciplinary overlap, depending on your area of speciality. Teach Spanish history or geography in a Spanish language lesson if you are a history or geography teacher. If you are ICT teacher, go to the computer workroom and use resources to teach anything remotely close to the assigned period while developing basic computer skills.

A whole school policy for homework

In any school, both teachers and parents need to know what is expected of students in the way of homework and how it should be organised and managed. The best way to ensure this is for schools to have a written policy on homework, publicly available on request. This policy is normally drawn up after careful consultation with all staff and parents and should be reviewed regularly. You should ask for this policy if you are undertaking long term supply. short term supply teachers are not normally required to mark homework in either primary or secondary schools. A good whole school policy, consistently applied, can ensure that homework arrangements are manageable for everyone, not least teachers. Two DfES consultation documents offer guidelines for schools on homework, one for primary school and one for secondary school. The full texts of the consultation documents are available from the DfES's main web site. www.dfes.gov.uk

Health and safety

The statement of Health and Safety applies to Science, Design and Technology, Information and Communication Technology, Art and Design, and Physical Education. When working with tools, equipment and materials, in practical activities and in different environments, some of them unfamiliar, students should be taught and adhere to: about hazards, risks and risk control. They should learn to recognize hazards, assess consequent risks and take steps to control the risks to themselves and others, and use information to assess the immediate and cumulative risks. They should also be taught to manage their environment to ensure the health and safety of themselves and others, explaining the steps they take to control risks. If you, as a short term supply teacher working a single day or a week, are requested to cover in such circumstances and are not competent in these areas, make this known as soon as possible. Classes can be re-housed to a room other than a lab. A school understands in placing the children's safety above other issues. There is no point in a teacher of English sitting with 25 children aged 15-16 in a wood-work lab if they do not know first aid or where the emergency electricity cut-off switches are or how to instruct a dyslexic child to drill holes in a sheet of plywood while keeping an eye on the other 24 children!

The National Literacy Strategy and the National Numeracy Strategy

The National Literacy Strategy and the National Numeracy Strategy are at the heart of the government's drive to raise standards in schools. The aim is to support teachers and others working in schools to improve literacy and numeracy for all children. The National Curriculum web site at www.nc.uk.net carries available guidance and documents about both the National Literacy Strategy and the National Numeracy Strategy. It provides direct access to professional development materials as well as information about new initiatives and events to support improvements in literacy and numeracy. As a supply teacher in primary schools this will form an essential part of every day of your teaching.

Key Stages 1 and 2 planning

The Education Act 1996, section 353b, defines a programme of study as the 'matters, skills and processes' that should be taught to students of different abilities and maturities during the key stage. The programme of study set out what students should be taught in each subject at each key stage, and provides the basis for planning schemes of work. The national frameworks for teaching literacy and mathematics published by the DfES and the exemplar schemes of work www.standards.dfes.gov.uk/schemes/, jointly published by the DfES and QCA, show how the programmes of study and attainment targets can be translated into practical, manageable teaching plans.

Supply teachers planning for schemes of work should start from the programmes of study and the needs and abilities of their students. Take note of EAL, SEN and Gifted and Talented children in your class. It is often not easy in mixed ability classes to be precise in your teaching planning and its implementation – flexibility and patience are needed to ensure that all the students are learning. You may have to cater for up to four different abilities in any given lesson, depending on the size of the school. Some schools stream their students into ability groups, where level descriptions can help to determine the degree of challenge and progression for work across each year of a key stage.

Key Stages 1 and 2 reporting

Teachers, including long term supply teachers, are required to report annually to parents on their children's progress. The level descriptions can be used as a basis to describe students' progress. short term supply teachers in primary schools are normally required to mark that day's work as well, but not homework. So be aware that your evaluations contribute to such reporting. Prepare a single side A4 report for the regular teacher, in addition to marking the children's exercise books. Note in the teacher report any exceptional children, any problematic children and any unusual observations. Sometimes a supply teacher sees things differently from a regular teacher who has become accustomed to a group – such as noting problems that are developing amongst children sitting at the back of the class. Move children around, even if there is a seating plan, to see if this makes a difference to children who appear to be disinterested or unsettled.

Key Stages 1 and 2 target setting

An attainment target sets out the 'knowledge, skills and understanding which students of different abilities and maturities are expected to have by the end of each key stage' as defined by the Education Act 1996, section 353a. These attainment targets consist of eight level descriptions of increasing difficulty, plus a description for exceptional performance above level 8. Each level description describes the types and range of performance that students working at that level should characteristically demonstrate. The level descriptions providing the basis for making judgements about students' performance at the end of key stages 1 and 2 can be found at www.nc.uk.net. Although the level descriptions are mainly used to assess attainment, you may also find them useful for lesson planning.

The government has established national targets for the proportion of 11-year-olds achieving level 4 in English and mathematics National Curriculum tests at the end of key stage 2. Schools are required to set targets for the proportions of their students reaching these targets. Optional tests in English and mathematics are available to assist schools in monitoring students' progress towards these targets. To prepare the children for these tests you can obtain previous year's tests and use them as practice tests. It is also advisable to look at the tests at the start of the year to see what level of teaching preparation you should aim for: pass level and top level. In doing so you should also be aware that for some aspects of statutory assessment in English and Mathematics at the end of key stage 1, level 2 has been subdivided into 2a, 2b, 2c to allow differentiation between student's attainment at level 2. To support target setting for students who achieve significantly below age-related expectations, performance criteria have also been developed in English and Mathematics leading to level 1 and within levels 1 and 2. In addition, performance criteria have been developed for students' personal and social development. These criteria were published in Supporting the target setting process (DfEE/QCA, 1998).

Key Stages 1 and 2 Religious education

Under the Education Act (1996) schools must provide Religious education for all registered students, although parents can choose to withdraw their children from these. Schools other than voluntary aided schools and those of a specific religious character must teach religious education according to the locally agreed syllabus. Each agreed syllabus should reflect the fact that the religious traditions in Great Britain are in the main Christian, while taking account of the teachings and practices of the other principal religions represented in Great Britain. A supply teacher is expected to behave on the same standard as that of a teacher hired on contract to a school and to be impartial and objective when teaching religious education.

On occasion I have taught in Church of England (CE) and Roman Catholic (RC) primary schools. Some of these schools have a policy to have a short prayer either during class registration, at the start of each lesson or during assembly. A daily supply teacher is not expected to be of the same faith as the school's denominations though it would be advisable if you intend to undertake long term cover to be comfortable about working in a school whose religious beliefs you don't share. There is no law to restrain you from doing long term supply in such schools but it is advisable to tell the school straight away that you are not of the same faith. Headteachers understand. It is more important to have an excellent Key Stage 1 or Key Stage 2 teacher than a teacher who has the same faith as the school. There is no point in creating a disturbance amongst the children by ignoring their requests to say a prayer, revealing that you do not know the words, or showing a dislike of a prayer. The school will make arrangements for someone else to conduct the prayer.

The majority of children in faith-based schools will be of its faith but generally not all. In some schools you may see children sitting elsewhere than in an assembly because their parents have requested exemption from prayer. Point this out to a regular teacher who will take the appropriate steps for ascertaining that they are exempt. Children may ask you questions if they think that you are not of the faith of the school. Be objective and if in doubt seek advice from the headteacher. This is an experience common to every supply teacher.

Certain state schools run by LEAs have predominate religions but are not operated or managed as faith schools. This is often the case in large urban areas, particularly those with large ethnic minority populations. The school may have a majority Muslim or Hindu composition. Virtually 100% could be members of a community that has immigrated to Britain to escape strife in their country, be it Bangladesh, Somalia, Turkey/Kurdistan, or Kosova. The school may thus follow traditions and practices in response to the request of the local community or religious leaders.

Sex and drug education

Primary and secondary schools must provide and keep up to date a written statement of their policy on sex education and make it available to parents and students. Schools must provide sex education and drugs education for their students. Sex education must include teaching about AIDS, HIV and other sexually transmitted infections and be given in such a way as to encourage students to have due regard to moral considerations and the value of family life. The detailed content and nature of sex education is for schools to decide. Parents can choose to withdraw their children from all or part of sex education.

Normally supply teachers will not be required to undertake such specialist teaching though each week schools normally set aside one lesson for Personal Social and Health Education (PSHE) and many primary schools now teach citizenship. This may include such topics as sex and drugs education or it may be discussions on voting, the role of governments and governance, or equal rights and opportunities. Schools usually bring in LEA or local Social Service specialist trained instructors or the school nurse. They are also likely to be the people who give education about drugs, although some schools use their local community police officer. The major pharmaceutical companies also send representatives to schools to demonstrate and to hand out hygiene and sanitary samples. Short and long term supply teachers can and will be asked to sit with a class during these lessons and demonstrations. Children may ask the supply teacher questions. If you are not certain of an answer, say so and refer the child to the relevant authority.

Homework

The DfES's guidance defines homework as any work or activities which students are asked to do outside lesson time. The main purposes of homework include: developing an effective partnership between the school and parents and other carers in pursuing the aims of the school – the purpose of home/school agreements; consolidating and reinforcing skills and understanding, particularly in literacy and numeracy; exploiting resources for learning, of all kinds, at home; extending school learning, for example through additional reading; encouraging students as they get older to develop the confidence and self-discipline needed to study on their own, and preparing them for the requirements of secondary school. This is vital given the importance of life long learning and adaptability.

A long term supply teacher is expected both to set and mark homework. The headteacher or line manager in charge of curriculum development will assist you in defining the amount of homework that can be set each week and the levels of expectation. The headteacher or line manager in charge of curriculum development will also be able to provide guidance on how to handle the failure of children to submit homework. There is a staged process that might eventually lead to consultation with parents or LEA Social Services. A short term supply teacher is not expected to mark homework but might be requested to set homework based on class work that has not been completed in a school day.

Key Stages 3 and 4 planning

Children sit the SATS examinations at the end of Year 6 and then leave primary school to enter secondary school. This is a dramatic change for them in learning as teaching is organized quite differently in the two sectors. A supply teacher should understand that planning for schemes of work for Key Stage 3 should start from the programmes of study and the needs and abilities of their students. Students also take a step forward when they move from Key Stage 3 to Key Stage 4 after the end of Year 9 SATS. Students in the two years of Key Stage 4 are expected to make decisions on the subjects in whom they wish to sit GCSE examinations at the end of Year 11. A supply teacher should be aware of children with EAL or SEN and those designated Gifted and Talented in the class.

Key Stages 3 and 4 reporting and target setting

At the end of Key Stage 3 and the end of Key Stage 4, the students sit SATS and GCSE examinations respectively. Criteria for target setting were published in Supporting the target setting process (DfEE/QCA 1998). As a long term supply teacher, you can obtain previous years' tests and use them to prepare the children for these tests. It is advisable to look at the tests at the start of the year to see what level of teaching preparation you should aim for – whether pass level or top level. Past tests are also a helpful exercise for a short term supply teacher to present to a class in the second and third term if no cover work has been set. You can spend half the lesson giving a short test from some of the questions and the other half going over the answers.

As well as the Year 9 SATS and Year 11 GCSE examinations, teachers are required to report annually to parents on their children's progress. short term supply teachers in secondary schools are not normally required to mark any class work or any homework. However, leave a brief report for the regular teacher noting any exceptional children, any problematic children and any unusual observation, as an informal way of contributing to student progress reports.

Long term supply teachers are required to mark class work as well as set and mark homework. The level descriptions provide the basis for making judgements about students' performance at the end of Key Stage 3. At Key Stage 4, national qualifications are the main means of assessing attainment in National Curriculum subjects. An exception is the case of Citizenship education where expected performance for the majority of students at the end of Key Stages 3 and 4 is set out in the end of key stage descriptions. The attainment targets and expected levels can be found at www.nc.uk.net

Secondary school Religious education

Under the Education Act 1996 schools must provide religious education for all registered students, although parents can choose to withdraw their children. Schools, other than voluntary aided schools and those of a religious character, must teach religious education according to the locally agreed syllabus. Each agreed syllabus should reflect the fact that the religious traditions in Great Britain are in the main Christian, while taking account of the teachings and practices of the other principal religions represented in Great Britain. A supply teacher is expected to be impartial and objective when teaching religious education, especially in secondary schools where they can face challenging questions and discussions.

Supply teachers should also be aware that some Church of England and Roman Catholic secondary schools have a policy to have a short prayer either during class registration, at the start of each lesson or during assembly. There is no law to restrain you from undertaking a long term assignment if you are not of these faiths. Headteachers are understanding that an excellent specialist subject teacher in Key Stage 3 and 4 is more important than being of the same faith as the schools' funding and governing authority.

I once went into an East London secondary school on a Friday in December and found that the school was not serving food that day and lunchtime had been reduced from its regular one hour to 30 minutes. This was because the student population was 100% Muslim, fasting for the month of Ramadan. The local leaders had requested that they be let out early to attend Friday prayers at sunset. The non-Muslim teaching staff, therefore, discreetly slipped off premises to have their lunch at the local café, and senior management detentions normally held on Fridays had been changed to Mondays. Supply teaching at such schools is an experience in diversity and should be enjoyed as such. Utilise such experiences to your benefit to build upon your strengths as a teacher.

Secondary school Careers education

All schools must provide a programme of Careers education for students during Years 9, 10 and 11 and an appropriate range of careers information. They must also allow officers from the careers service access to students at key decision-making points during their schooling. DfES circulars 5/97 and 5/98 provide guidance for schools on meeting the statutory requirements. To complement these the QCA has also published guidance for schools and colleges *Learning outcomes from careers education and guidance* (QCA/99/359).

Your own experiences as a supply teacher, whether from other parts of the world or as a NQT, is a welcome contribution to any school. As a UK trained NQT you are probably the closest in age to these students. You might interest them in your recent decisions taking you towards university and a career in teaching, explaining why you have chosen this path. As a non-UK trained supply teacher you should be valued as someone who can explain situations in other countries, and can advise on careers that have local or global options for work and other short term programmes such as a gap year in your home country. Supply teachers on short term assignments would do well to prepare a few lessons around careers. If no cover has been set for a lesson, ask permission to give a careers lesson. Schools are normally pleased to agree, seeing this is constructive use of time. As a supply teacher on a long term assignment it is expected of you to coordinate with other teachers.

Possible modifications at Key Stage 4

A supply teacher should be aware that Regulations under section 363 of the 1996 Education Act allow schools to make exceptional provision to meet a wider range of individual students' needs. From September 2000, regulations allow schools to meet the statutory requirement for students to study Design and Technology, modern foreign languages or Science by providing courses leading to a specified range of qualifications, not all of which will fully cover the programmes of study. The range of qualifications is separately specified in the annual DfES circular listing qualifications approved under section 400 of the 1996 Education Act.

Schools may disapply, for any one student, up to two National Curriculum subjects, in order to: provide wider opportunities for work-related learning than are possible alongside the full statutory requirement by disapplying up to two of Design and Technology, modern foreign languages and Science; allow students making significantly less progress than their peers to study fewer National Curriculum subjects in order to consolidate their learning across the curriculum by disapplying Design and Technology and/or modern foreign languages; respond to students' individual strengths and talents by allowing them to emphasise a particular curriculum area by exchanging a statutory subject for a further course in that curriculum area, by disapplying Design and Technology and/or modern foreign languages. Guidance is available in: Disapplication of the National Curriculum at Key Stage 4 using section 363 of the 1996 Education Act for a wider focus on work-related learning (order ref. QCA/98/215).

As a supply teacher you should know how to implement the above in the classroom, so spend a weekend online at www.standards.dfee.gov.uk/schemes/ and look at all the schemes of work. Your assignment on a short term supply cover could be 'General Cover – no work set' whereas on a long term cover you may have children who float around the school with a different timetable to their normal year group. Be aware and able to cope with such circumstances.

So you know that supply teaching is still teaching in theory: but what really happens in a school and the classroom?

6

The School and the Classroom

Proper preparation for supply teaching is essential, as the students need to be learning. This entails more than you knowing the National Curriculum and having taken professional development courses. How you prepare between your arrival time at the school and the start of the lessons can be essential to the smooth functioning of your classroom. Taking the correct supplies into the classroom can add an extra five minutes to your teaching opportunity. Try be early but not too early. Be at the school at least half an hour earlier than the start of the first lesson. There is much to do before you start your first class. You need to find the school, find the parking lot, find a parking space, find the room where you are to teach, find the lesson plans, reviewing the material you are to teach, familiarise yourself with school procedures, and plan your own teaching strategy for the course you will be teaching.

Supply can be rewarding but it is hard work. When I was student teacher and then a full-time teacher on contract with a school I was able to spend time with the students and develop rapport with them. A supply is in and out. Usually it's a one-day shot. The children don't know you, and you don't know them. They are used to their classroom teacher, and then they get this stranger for one day. So you have to establish rapport in one day to achieve educational results. This is easier in primary school where you are with the same children in every lesson. In a secondary school frequent use of daily supply teachers for different subjects may have generated disruption that can become more than some children want to handle. A teacher cannot be expected to establish a working rapport with every student in one hour, given that this might be the only hour that they might work together. Expect and plan for the worst and savour anything that turns out better.

You know you are faced with a system that tends to isolate you. You may be king or queen of the class but in schools, places that exist to disseminate knowledge, a supply teacher has only a short time, often minutes, before lessons start to find out what to teach, although some schools have developed effective team approaches to teaching. The supply teacher will rarely if ever get feedback on performance the way a regular teacher will, from lesson observations by senior management. This isolation not only denies a supply teacher the chance to improve performance by learning from experience, it also fosters a debilitating isolation that could lead to stress and burnout.

Educators are facing new pressures that make it more crucial than ever for supply teachers to learn the strategies and methods that make for higher quality instruction. The DfES has mandates for schools to raise student academic performance to higher standards, as well as providing drug education, having policies on violence and sexual harassment. Increased demands result from dwindling public confidence and tax resources – but how does a supply teacher attain all this with only one foot in the door? Some supply agencies have introduced mentoring systems but it may well be the case of too little too late. My mentor at my supply agency is burdened with a potential 250 supply teachers who might all call him on the same night – yet we are all too tired after school to do so.

If that isn't tough enough, the regular classroom teacher might be unhappy with what they find when they return. It is not unheard of for them to request that the supply teacher NEVER sets foot in their room again. The flip side is, if they are happy with what they find when they return, they will personally request the same supply teacher the next time they have to be absent. Your frequency of supply teaching depends on your efforts in a school and the children's and school's happiness with your efforts. So entering any school for the first time is a daunting experience.

Who is in charge when you arrive and what do you do

In primary schools, a short term supply teacher will normally report to the headteacher, and in secondary schools to a deputy headteacher or assistant headteacher. Long term supply teachers in both primary and secondary are subject to the normal managerial structure of head of year, head of department/subject and/or line manager. The rule of thumb for matters inside a classroom is head of department/subject including disciplinary referrals. For matters outside of classroom disciplinary referrals are to head of form/year. Supply teachers who develop a powerful bond with these people derive benefits that last well past their first day on the job. short term supply teaching can become long term supply teaching or even a contract with a school. A supportive senior can play a key role in helping supply teachers find a new meaning to their careers, take part in professional development, and make full use of planning time.

Remember your virtues and professional qualities as a nomadic teacher when you arrive at a school to find the person in charge. Sign the visitor's register, which also serves as the fire register and, should the need arise, as proof that you arrived and left school on time. Ask for the person in charge of cover or supply teachers. There may only be a few minutes at the start of a day for the supply teacher to get the keys, school map, register and if possibly set work. You may be one of many daily short term supply teachers who all need to be attended to in a very short time. The person in charge is often under stress. Setting a cover list also entails dealing with regular staff who might have to cover a lesson or two in the day and are reluctant to do so.

The school administrator – success starts at the top

Educational administrators who hire supply teachers have an extremely important job. They have the responsibility of placing a qualified professional into every classroom. There are many factors important for school effectiveness and supply teacher quality is a major one. Good educational administrators want to ensure the academic success of all children. Education is not an exact science and the qualities that are needed in supply teaching personnel will vary somewhat depending on the objectives and needs of the school. The person in charge should also be accessible, not just someone in the building.

Supply teachers want a place to send children who are making it difficult for others to learn, so that they can focus on teaching. And supply teachers want the disciplinary process to have some teeth. Students need to know that the headteacher is supporting you. You lose credibility when you send a student to the office, and they come back without having been disciplined. Supply teachers also lose credibility when they send students to the office too often for things they should deal with themselves. Major discipline problems can often be avoided by seeking help early on when the problems are easier to solve. Don't get stressed and blame yourself if things get out of hand in your classroom because a school does not have 'success at the top'. Grin and bear the situation for the day and politely tell your supply agency that afternoon that you are not willing to return to that school. You will not be the first to decline a supply teaching assignment there.

Encouraging best practice in the school: am I wanted back, do I get feedback?

'I've always been in demand, so I must be doing something right' is the boast of one supply teacher to another. Supply teachers should accept that an invitation to return to the school signifies approval. If a school decides not to ask you back, it doesn't usually inform you of that decision. So if it offers no further work you will not know whether you were not wanted back, or were simply not needed. This system, which is designed to protect the interests of students, works well in the situation where a supply teacher is deemed to be competent. Repeated offers of work enable a supply teacher to become more familiar with the working situation and develop closer links with colleagues. This gives rise to enhanced professional confidence and competence in that setting and can produce fruitful working relationships to the benefit of all involved. The system is more problematic if the supply teacher is disliked, for whatever reason. The school is not obliged to inform the supply teacher if it is dissatisfied, so the teacher will remain unaware of the dissatisfaction and might well repeat the same mistakes in other schools, to the probable detriment of the students.

The challenge for supply teachers is to prevent a dampening of students' enthusiasm. Supply teachers sometimes feel they should not push – shouldn't rock the boat. This isn't great advice for teachers. We all rock the boat. Every day, supply teachers take risks and deal with them. Being assigned a school of challenging students with complicated learning needs could be overwhelming, especially if you don't know in advance that they are the most challenging students in the city and you arrive to find the school surrounded by barbed wire and having its own resident Police Officer. Rock the boat – but politely. Calmly ask for a SEN/EAL register. Ask the person in charge of supply to point out children who have learning or social problems or a criminal record. Ask the person in charge of supply at a school for any specific assistance you need. It will make your job that much easier in terms of discipline so that you can actually teach, which is what the school is paying you to do. At the end of the day, the school and the children will appreciate you for your efforts – even if you go home exhausted.

Remember that schools usually do not have written policies regarding their deployment of supply teachers. Supply teachers have to be flexible, adaptable. You have to be able to fit in as quickly as possible, stand on your own feet as quickly as possible, become a member of the department as quickly as possible. You have to prove yourself straight away – if you aren't good at the start they won't have you back.

You are not normally aware of the school's special problem children nor of its best practice. The daily supply teacher is not normally given a SEN/EAL register, unless it is requested. It is highly unlikely that a short term supply teacher will attend any form of School meeting whereas a long term supply teacher may need to attend fortnightly lesson planning meetings with other teachers in the same subject and the head of department/subject. At best, by arriving early, you may be given an insight into the school and its best practice at a staff-room meeting before the start of the lessons, depending on the school.

The substance of supply teaching
Schools employ supply teachers precisely because they are so busy and short of staff, or to create some free time for development work. So devoting large amounts of time to producing detailed notes for the supply teacher can seem to them onerous or even counter-productive. This creates a dichotomy at the point of transfer of responsibility – there is a conflict of interests between the supply teacher who needs information and the absent or non-existent colleague who is not providing such notes. If in doubt and where no help is forthcoming, a supply teacher should turn to a more back-to-basics approach. Complicated

pedagogical strategies have no meaning to a class that has never met you. Children are inquisitive – direct this towards you and your topic. Involve the children in questions and answers. Avoid a lecture. It is advisable to create a sense of well being. Show you have nothing to hide. Answer questions about where you are from or what football team you support, but not about personal matters. Aim to build up the children's excitement and subsequent accomplishment in learning from your experience once you have established rapport.

Supply teachers should note the importance of discussing curriculum and problems with teachers, including other supply teachers. Professional development for a supply teacher is as vital as for any other teacher. This may mean working long hours during and after school and depleting your creative energy trying to reinvent the wheel. Children are perceptive and will soon see through a teacher who is old hat or simply handing out worksheets. Don't forget you may be standing in for their regular five-star teacher who is on a day's INSET.

A regular teacher relies on the fact that parental involvement in education – at home and in the classroom – is vital to effective learning and discipline. If parents back a teacher's discipline of a student, and the parent restricts privileges at home, the teacher notices real improvements in the student. A supply teacher cannot rely on such cooperation.

So what do you do? Ask for advice! Ask a child to show you what they did the previous day and carry on with the same set of work – continuity is the name of the game. Follow procedures if discipline begins to deteriorate. Schools suggest two oral warnings to a bad apple student, then to tell them to stand outside the door for five minutes then come back in. This is a legal requirement.

Don't show your anger – be calm and objective. Use short sentences. Don't enter into an argument. The problem student is not picking on you so don't take it personally. The student may have serious problems at home and the last thing needed is anger from a strange teacher. The problem student may only be seeking attention. If the oral warnings fail, then send another student to get help from the school office – schools usually have on-call systems from senior management for discipline problems. Your job is to teach as many children as much as possible in any given period. Do so and the school will ask for you to come back again.

The students' perspective on supply teachers

That the first day may be the last for the supply teacher has to be faced by the students as well. There is no fixed rule on what to expect. A long term assignment supply teacher often encounters antagonism by school children who like the 'real teacher' who has gone sick or on maternity leave. Moreover, some students equate the word supply with party-time. Other students, however, can be tremendously helpful to their visitor. The children's favourite teacher is their regular one, if they have one.

You will find that constant short term supply in the same classroom generates unease and curiosity among the young children. Be positive even in the midst of mindless behaviour, whether paper-aircraft throwing, eating breakfast and lunch in front of you, crawling across tables or the occasional fistfight. This may just be a baptism of fire to test how far they can go. Sarcasm does not help – saying 'You are such a wonderful class, your parents and school should really be proud!' will only generate confusion. Use the principle of divide and rule. Gather those who are sitting quietly and with their books out, towards the front of the class. Shift some tables and chairs in a circle at the back of the class. Just this act will gather everyone together to help out of curiosity. Then start with some group work. Show an interest. Bring in a 'well-done' rubber stamp or stickers. Put up a star-chart in the classroom. The carrot is mightier than the stick!

Show an interest in the students' homework, as it's part of your job to motivate their learning. At the various Key Stages, the National Curriculum suggests the number of hours of homework to be set for each student in each subject. Schools often determine a homework day for each subject to spread the workload. Parents know this and they want to see their children doing homework. Parents like children coming home and telling them that their teacher told them 'well done'. Children, especially in primary schools, will give you homework completed the previous night at the start of the lesson. Be positive – thank the children, congratulate them. If you feel confident with the subject, spend some time going over the homework on the board. Not every lesson and all of every lesson has to be innovatively new. Reinforce their previous knowledge.

Don't balk at your obligations. In primary schools on short term supply you are not required to mark homework, though you are required to mark class-work. In primary schools on short term supply you are not required to set homework if homework has not been set by the regular teacher. On short term supply in secondary schools you are not required to mark homework, neither are you required to mark class-work nor to set homework if homework has not been set by the regular teacher. If homework has been set, however, ensure that it is written down in the students' planner/diary. Not all children volunteer to be diligent. Be consistent and fair in handling the students. Never lose your temper over class-work or homework that has not been done. If you are on short term supply, leave a note for the regular teacher; if on long term supply tell the head of form/year.

Classroom survival tips

The starting bell has rung for the first lesson. Your ability to handle a class smoothly comes from confidence in knowing that you have successfully navigated the minefield of the nomadic bureaucracy and lifestyle outside the classroom. You can now focus your undivided attention on teaching. Apply these general principles and you will survive as a supply teacher but basic survival is not enough. Say it to yourself *'Basic survival is not enough'*. You want ultimate survival. Take note of these tips:

There are no kids in your class, only students. The students in your class will be whatever you want them to be. If you call them 'kids', they will act like kids. If you call them 'students', they are more likely to act maturely and learn. So treat students with respect. Respect breeds respect – this includes 'hearing' every question, giving praise for students' work, and allowing all students to participate.

Being fair or consistent is a utopian goal. As a supply teacher in over 60 schools I have tried to be fair and consistent, I have tried to give students chances to redeem themselves – but this doesn't always work. It's ironic: you need a firm hand; you need to spot the troublemaker right away or your classroom can descend into chaos. If you focus on what you want, the room is the way you'd like it to be and the majority of the class are well behaved, considerate, and enjoying learning something, you have succeeded. Democracy does work in utopia.

Have students doing something at all times. A plan is vital! Having no plan is giving students free rein in the classroom, and this is never a good idea. An assignment should be written on the chalkboard. Tell students to work silently, and to complete the work in a given time. This assignment can be anything appropriate.

Show enthusiasm. If you are enthusiastic about teaching, show it! Make learning fun. Your eagerness for teaching will increase the motivation of your students. It helps build a sense of teamwork. Enthusiasm is contagious.

Born to teach – it's a myth that only certain types of people are born with the ability to command, gain the students' respect, and have good classroom discipline. The classroom is the place where the supply teacher blossoms. The supply's attitude and ability flourish in front of the class. Your very personality is put on display in front of students. The teaching methods are up to you and the teaching plans are sometimes of your choice.

Know your content. Keep up with changes in the National Curriculum. Keep up with new books and resources. Look over each year's exam papers. No matter if this is your first year of teaching or your thirtieth, keep up with changing trends in your field of expertise.

Be alert to your surroundings. A supply teacher should always be aware of what is happening with their students. This includes foreground activities, background activities, and activities not directly under your control but still your responsibility. You may want to devote more time to watching the student who repeatedly asks to go to the toilet than the other students in the classroom.

Be organized: efficient organization allows you to spend more learning time with students. Have a way of handling routines – collecting student work, handing out materials, posting assignments, what to do when finished with an assignment, communicating class news, etc. Established routines keep the class on track and give you more time for teaching and engaging students.

Skip the coffee. Even though coffee is a breakfast item, try to skip it. Coffee is the supply teacher's enemy. It raises the probability of needing to use the restroom. Sometimes the day is arranged so that it is two hours before you will be able to.

Make a pass with your name on it and take it to every class where you teach. If you must stop a lesson to write a pass, it hinders the steady flow of the classroom dynamic. It's worth putting your pass on cardboard or heavy paper. These can be computer generated or hand-written one minute before class begins. Make sure you get the pass back from students who use it and always have a spare one.

Teach actively. Headteachers, like other supervisors and managers of people, appreciate those who work hard. Effective teachers are involved, they move around, they don't stand around but are busy. They are actively involved with students and with other staff.

Politeness and continuity: the class that was so well mannered and polite yesterday can be obnoxious and impolite today. And there will be days when you will feel obnoxious and impolite, too. But you must exhibit constant behaviour. The life of a student is unstable and ever changing: the students don't need a supply teacher who is the same. Listen to what you say to others and the tone of voice you use. You should be expressing care, concern and respect.

The leader of the pack. There is always one student who wanders into class long before anyone else does. Speaking with this student is the best insurance a supply teacher can get, and it is free for the taking. The two minutes you spend speaking to this student can forewarn you of problems that will need to be dealt with. This student may tell you about in-class rivalries between two students that often turn violent when a supply teacher is in charge. Or maybe about the usual trick the students repeatedly play on supply teachers. The early student might mention the Assembly during third period that nobody has told you about, or how James and Jennifer have epileptic seizures but that the students know how to deal with this.

Never assume that the day will go smoothly. Have a back-up plan. Use your back-up teaching plan when the absent teacher doesn't leave a set of lesson plans for the day. The primary supply teacher should have at least one plan for a literacy class, at least one plan for a numeracy class. The secondary teacher should have a plan to involve children in a group activity that could be generic, for example 'discuss pollution' – which would apply to history, geography, science and even English and ICT by requiring the writing and typing of a report. Every supply teacher should plan for days when they know nothing about the subject for class they are teaching and no lesson plans have been left for them. Usually this is known as general cover.

Doing general cover generally means that the school really needs someone in the classroom to maintain good order and discipline so they do not have to send the children home. Get used to the reality of day-to-day cover since you may cover six different subjects in six different periods in a single day. This can sometimes be enjoyable – like teaching primary school but at a secondary school!

Establish successful classroom management. Set up and enforce your classroom management system from the first lesson. Discipline and reasonable structure are essential for students to be on task and to have an orderly class environment. Avoid making rules that you do not enforce, for students will soon learn that what you say does not matter.

Show confidence. Anxiety can take many forms: stuttering, looking off in the distance when asked a tough question, staring, twitching, frantically searching for a piece of chalk, or the most blatant form of 'sweating' – responding 'I don't know' to a question asked by a student. If you don't know then say 'what do you think?' and 'let's look that up together.'

Smiling can often be mistaken by students for 'sweating'. Avoid this confusion by not smiling until the students are doing what they should be doing, and you are in control of the classroom.

Pace the instruction. The amount learned is related to the opportunity to learn. Students learn most by doing, not by watching, not by standing in line, and not by listening. Plan an instructional time line for your courses. Nothing is worse than approaching the end of the school day or the end of the school year and realizing there is not enough time to finish the full course of study.

You are the King or Queen of the castle. You have been given control of the classroom: make it yours. The class will challenge this control. Making your acceptable noise level known can take many forms – wait for the children to come to you – don't shout out 'keep quiet' as this will be drowned by their noise and only raise your blood pressure.

Maintain good interpersonal skills: work well with others. Headteachers need supply teachers who work well with others. If people don't like your behaviour as a teacher, they will not want to be around you. This is true of colleagues and parents as well as students. Education is a people business. Good human relations skills are imperative for teachers.

Communicate clearly so the students can learn. Effective supply teachers give information clearly. Be concise. Demonstrate as well as explain. When presenting new information teachers must give accurate directions. This includes explaining, outlining, summarizing and reviewing. Too often children have no idea what they are supposed to be learning or why they are learning it.

Be flexible not brittle. Being a supply teacher and being flexible are one and the same. You must be willing to teach a boys' PE class, even though the supply agency consultant called you in to supply for a Maths class. You must be flexible when your lunch break is cancelled because they need a stand-in security person for the noon-hour rave dance contest the Music Department is sponsoring. If you are not flexible, the school may have a hard time effectively utilizing your talents. As the saying goes, 'the flexible shall not be bent out of shape.'

Question effectively. Questioning is a powerful teaching tool. It is through questioning that productive thinking is generated. Ask questions directed to the whole class as well as to individuals. When directing a question to an individual student, ask the question first before calling on a student. Give time for students to think through their responses. Do not call on them by name too soon. The children know that you don't know them and are working from a class register. This wait time keeps everyone involved and gives the students a chance to think. It takes nerve to wait, but many successful supply teachers use the method effectively.

Remember a sleeping student is a blessing. Let them sleep. There is a reason the student is sleeping, and chances are good that this reason has very little to do with you. Waking the student will stop the flow of the class and, assuming you are successful, they will learn very little, and may cause havoc in the classroom. On the other hand, a sleeping student isn't learning.

Differentiate instruction: One of the biggest challenges to supply teaching is working with students who have varying learning styles, personalities and rates of learning and keeping them all learning. Supply teachers need to mix auditory, visual and hands-on techniques. For specific lessons, group students with similar weaknesses or skill gaps.

Make them your students. Don't create a wall between the students and yourself. Be one with them. This means that you and the students are on the same side. That you laugh at the same jokes, know the same language and, together, will arrive at the same learning. The students pick up on this attitude, and are more willing to learn from you once they become *your* students.

Build success into your class. Regular success is important. If work is continuously too hard for students, they can become frustrated, provoking behaviour problems and loss of effort. When students are not successful, provide further instruction and/or simplify the task until they can master it and experience some success.

Walk around the class. You are the captain of this ship. Know what goes on aboard. Be aware of any actions that may call for your intervention. Walking around class reminds students whose ship it is. And it allows you to speak to the students, for both control and social purposes. If time and discipline permit, you can mark books while walking around. Praise the hard workers. Have a rubber stamp or stars for their homework diaries/planners. Chastise the lazy, but do it politely.

Hold high expectations. Headteachers want supply teachers who expect their students to learn. High expectations need to be communicated for good performance. Successful supply teachers don't just accept participation but also require it. One can be demanding without being unpleasant or mean. In fact, students respect supply teachers who expect them to do their best.

Meet the troublemakers face-to-face. If you ignore them, they seldom go away. One effective way to deal with troublemakers is to pick them out of the crowd and let it be known that you will be watching them. But this is tricky, as an exposed troublemaker can sometimes be a bigger problem than an invisible troublemaker. Experience will dictate the best method of discipline in each case.

Create a pleasant atmosphere for the students' learning. Don't allow your classroom to give out the aura of the haunted house on the hill. Dismal, drab and dreary environments reduce learning. Cheerful and happy classrooms will stimulate learning. Supply teachers don't have to create magic kingdoms in a single day to promote learning, but a pleasant room where students feel comfortable is a must for turning up the academic burner.

Permit a privilege and threaten to take it away. This is a backhanded method of controlling a class. You give the class a privilege that they don't normally get, and instruct them that the privilege will be allowed only as long as the class obeys your classroom rules.

Give students responsibility for discipline. This is an ingenious trick that works best with younger children. Divide the class into groups, and offer a reward for the best behaved group. This diverts any hostility away from you, and gets the students actively disciplining each other. Rewards for the groups are, for instance: using the computer first, being able to line up first for lunch, being able to choose their own team's activity for PE, etc. Students will tell you the reward they most desire.

Use sound effects. Everyone enjoys this technique for reading poems, or stories. Take apart a poem and write a sound script. Have students supply sound for the different moods of the poem. Not only will students enjoy reading poems more, but they will look forward to reading poems in the future. Some students may even script the next poem for you.

Look like a teacher, act like a teacher. The students and the school expect a supply teacher to be professional. This means dressing, talking, and acting professionally. This rules out dressing in blue jeans and T-shirt, and cursing. So follow school rules. Different schools have different rules. It is your duty to know and abide by the rules of each school you work in.

Build a school checklist

Keeping all these survival tips in your head is not easy. What you need is a quick checklist that will soon become routine, especially if you are doing supply teaching on a regular basis. Having met the person in charge when you arrive at the school, you should be given certain information, particularly if you have not done supply work at the school before. If you are not provided with the following information then you should ask for it. Not every point on the checklist will apply in all situations. In particular, the distinction between doing supply work in the primary and secondary sectors is taken into account.

- ☐ Who arranges supply cover and who is to be your line manager – you may go to a class to find no one there or the wrong group.

- ☐ Who signs your timesheets at the end of the day or the end of the week?

- ☐ What are the names of the head of department, key stage and subject co-ordinators and senior management team? Where can they be found at break times? You would like to teach content and need to know what the students are supposed to be learning.

- ☐ When can you take a class to the library or IT suite?

- ☐ Who do you contact in an emergency? And how? Children fight, ceilings leak, asthmatics lose their inhalers and so on.

- ☐ What are the timings of the school day and how are they indicated? Do bells mark the end of lessons and school sessions?

- ☐ What time are staff expected to arrive and leave? Remember primary school teachers are expected to mark that day's work.

- ☐ What are the arrangements for assembly and registration? Remember, if you are doing registration in primary school you must ask and pass on the information. Who gets school meals/ packed lunches/paying for their meals? Who takes the required money?

- ☐ Are you expected to do extra duties, e.g. break duty? If so, will you get paid for it? If not, should you be paid? Remember that in the eyes of the law you are a temporary worker. The DTI Work Time Initiative (1998) states, inter alia that you must get a 20-minute paid break for every two hours worked and a one-hour lunch break.

- ☐ Are you expected to attend staff training days, staff meetings and parents' evenings as a long term supply teacher? Again, will you – and should you – be paid?

- ☐ Is there any information about the layout of the school – where are the fire routes, are doors and toilets locked during lesson time, do certain staircases only give access to certain class-rooms?

☐ Is there a plan or map showing the location of rooms? If so, you should receive a copy. Where are the classrooms/teaching spaces – do you need a key for these?

☐ Where is the staff-room, cloakroom and lavatory – do you need a key for these?

☐ Is there any information about lesson routine? For example, are classrooms locked at the end of a school session? Do students line up outside the classroom before the lesson commences? Is there a seating plan for the classroom or are students able to choose their own seats?

☐ Have you been provided with a list of the students in the class you are covering? Do you call a register every lesson or take names on a piece of paper?

☐ Have you been told whether there are any children who have special educational needs? Are there any statemented students? From whom do you get this information?

☐ Has work been set for the class or classes you are covering and, if so, where can it be located? Are you expected to set work yourself? Are you expected to teach students or are you super-vising lessons only? If you are expected to teach a group of students, have you been provided with any or sufficient infor-mation about, for example, teaching resources? It will not be appropriate for you to be asked to carry out certain teaching tasks if you do not have the relevant qualifications and ex-perience, for example supervising science practical lessons and PE.

☐ Should students have certain books (for example, a textbook, exercise book, organiser or planner for homework) and equip-ment (for example, a pen or pencil) with them? Do you record their work in exercise books, on paper, or in some other way?

☐ Is there any guidance about marking, recording and assessment (if this is appropriate to the supply assignment)?

☐ What are the arrangements for dealing with student indiscipline and disruption – what is the school's discipline policy?

☐ Are any ancillary or support staff to work in the classroom while you teach? Are they in the classroom to support a specific student or are they to be deployed, as you deem appropriate?

☐ Do any of the students have medical conditions of which you should be aware? Will you be asked to administer any medication? (You are not contractually obliged to give medication or supervise students taking it.)

☐ What are the arrangements when a child is sick?

☐ What are the arrangements for wet weather?

☐ What are the procedures if there is an emergency – for example a fire?

☐ Is there a dress code (or other codes) that concerns you as a teacher? Is there a school uniform?

☐ What resources are available for you to use that are not in every class – such as photocopier, video machine? Supply teachers also need support to obtain needed supplies. Many struggle to get the materials they need.

☐ Finally, teachers want you to help them secure another key resource – time. Supply teachers are expected to teach a full schedule of classes, which doesn't leave time to prepare better labs or have someone show you how to incorporate an Internet site into a lesson. If new teachers didn't have a full schedule of classes, we wouldn't see so many teachers leaving the profession in the first years because they wouldn't feel so stressed out. Point out that if you don't get the chalk or white board marker then you cannot teach.

Classroom checklist

☐ Always, *always*, follow the classroom teacher's lesson plans or whatever instructions they have left. The major complaint I hear from teachers about supply is that they do not follow the lesson plans.

☐ Take time before school to review material that is unfamiliar. If that still does not help, try to find another teacher who will explain it to you. The second most frequent complaint I hear from teachers about supply is that they did not know anything about the subject, and confused the students. Make every attempt to understand the lessons.

☐ Make a discipline plan. Get input from the person in charge before you enter the classroom. Then follow through with it in the classroom. Another common complaint about supply is lack of classroom control. I have two 'rule' posters; one for primary and another for secondary. I suggest you have a maximum of five rules. I post the rules at the front of classroom before the students arrive. Often students will see my rule poster as they enter the room, and ask about it. At the start of class I explain each rule, and tell them the consequences of breaking the rules. The rules posted are the rules for as long as I am their supply – and it works.

☐ Bring some enjoyable extra things the students can do when, and only when, their work is completed. The students need to be learning. I bring 'fun sheets' for primary school students. Fun sheets can be pictures to colour, dot-to-dots, word searches, mazes, or something else along that line. For secondary school students I bring word puzzles and magazines.

☐ Leave a note for the regular teacher or headteacher at the end of the day. Let the classroom teacher know how the day went. Did the students struggle with a lesson? If so, let the teacher know. Did the students have fun with an activity? Again, let the teacher know. Remember to include the positives of the day as well as the negatives.

☐ Make sure the room is in order before leaving. Another common complaint is that the teacher can never find books and papers when they return. Make an effort to stack handed-in assignments in a neat and organized manner where the teacher can easily find them. Put all books away where they were at the start of the day. Be sure the room in general looks orderly.

Keep your spirits up and may the force be with you!

Postscript

Preparing for a supply day is nothing less than preparation for battle. Students you have never met before need to learn from you. As a supply teacher you should set up your own routine of handling a new school and a new classroom. One of your main responsibilities is keeping control of the classroom. Some days, this will be your only duty. Students will try to get at you in every way possible: if you leave a window of opportunity, they will take advantage of it. Before you step into a classroom, you must prepare yourself for battle – in the way you dress, the way you speak, and your knowledge of the class subject.

Your voice is very important to your role as a supply teacher and so is what you say. The first ten words out of your mouth will determine how the rest of the class runs. Before you set foot in a classroom, decide how you want your class to see you, and, with a cassette recorder, practise in advance being this person.

All forms of classroom teaching seem to involve three elements: a teacher, one who possesses certain knowledge on a specific topic; the specific topic to be taught; and a student, one who stands in need of the knowledge that the teacher possesses. Good supply teaching requires various combinations and permutations of the characteristics of these elements. Being prepared means you can teach and that you and your new class can enjoy yourselves. This approach has certainly made supply teaching easier and more enjoyable for me.

Know your place in the staff-room and remind other teachers. Use a whisper if need be – 'I am a guest here, trying to help you and the children – please what do I do next – may I please use the photocopier – is the coffee and tea free?'

At the end of the day you may be lucky enough to get a thank-you from the person in charge at a school but don't expect it as most are usually too exhausted. Simply get your time sheet signed, smile and head for the nearest telephone to contact your supply consultant in the LEA or the supply agency. You chose this nomadic life-style and there are students who need to be learning.

Terminology and Acronyms

Admission Authority – sets the criteria and makes the arrangements for admissions to school. In Community schools this is the LEA. In Voluntary Aided schools it is the governing body.

Agreed syllabus – a syllabus of Religious education that is not specific to one religion, adopted by an LEA for teaching in community and controlled schools. The course is developed by the SACRE (see below).

Appraisal – the process of assessing how well a member of staff is carrying out his or her job.

Attainment targets – the knowledge, skills and understanding which students of differing ability and maturity are expected to have by the end of each Key Stage of the National Curriculum.

Audit Commission – independent body set up by Government to monitor the use of funds by local authorities and certain other bodies.

ATL – Association of Teachers and Lecturers.

AWPU – Age-Weighted Student Unit. The sum of money allocated to the school for each student according to age. This is the basic unit of funding for the school.

Ballot – a method of voting, normally secret.

Baseline assessment – Assessment of student's attainment at entry to school (usually in the reception class or Year 1.

Behaviour Support Plan – Each LEA must produce a document outlining their policy and arrangements for supporting students with behavioural difficulties.

Benchmarking – The process of comparing the outcomes of an organisation or its processes to comparable organisations or other reference points such as national or regional data.

107

Bill – A draft of an act of Parliament, presented to either the House of Commons or the House of Lords, to vote on. If successful, the bill becomes an Act after Royal Assent.

Catchment Area – a defined geographical area from which a school takes its students.

Capital expenditure – spending on building projects and large items of equipment.

Casting vote – an additional vote to be used by the chair of governors if an equal number of votes is cast for and against a motion.

Circular – policy statement issued by a government department, which does not have the status of law, but which gives guidance on interpretation and implementation of the law.

Clerk to the governing body – a person appointed to carry out administrative duties for the governing body such as preparing an agenda, minuting meetings and dealing with correspondence.

Code of Practice published in 1994 to guide schools in how to identify and provide support for children with special educational needs. A revised version will be published in 2002.

Collective Worship – a statutory requirement in all maintained schools. Parents do have the right to withdraw their children from Collective worship.

Community school – School committed to life-long learning and involving the whole community.

Contingency fund – money set aside for unexpected costs.

Co-opted governor – a governor chosen by members of a governing body who have themselves been elected or appointed.

Core curriculum – English, Mathematics and Science – those subjects which must be studied by all students. Also called core subjects.

Current expenditure – spending on the day-to-day running of schools, including staff costs, heating and lighting, consumables etc; sometimes also called re-current expenditure.

Delegation – a process where one body or person gives another body or person authority to take decisions on a particular matter.

Department for Education and Skills (DfES) – central government department with responsibility for education.

Differentiation – the organisation of teaching programmes and methods specifically to suit the age, ability and aptitudes of individual children.

Disapplication – term used where parts of the National Curriculum requirements are lifted or modified in relation to a student in specified cases or circumstances.

Dual use – the use of any part of school premises by community groups and others, whether during or outside of school hours.

EAL – English as an Additional Language. English as a second language (ESL) was the term used previously.

Early years/foundation stage – Period of learning for children from aged 3 to the end of the school reception year.

EBD – Emotional and Behavioural Difficulties.

EAZ – Education Action Zone – a grouping of schools with additional resources thorough Public/Private funding, targeted at specific projects aimed at raising standards. Established EAZs are continuing but no new ones will be formed.

EDP – Education Development Plan which all LEAs are required to prepare.

EPS – Educational Psychological Service.

EWO – Education Welfare Officer. Deals with attendance problems and other welfare matters in co-operation with the school

Exclusion – banning a student from school by the headteacher, either temporarily or permanently, on disciplinary grounds.

Excellence in Cities – government programme targeted at supporting inner-city schools.

Fair Funding – a policy adopted by the headteacher for hiring out the use of any part of school premises by external groups.

Form 7 – A form submitted by every school each January to record the number of teachers employed, the number of children in each age group, the organisation of classes and so on.

Form of entry – number of classes that a school admits each year.

Formula funding – the method by which funds for school budgets are calculated. The most important factor is the number of students.

Foundation governor – a person appointed to be a member of a school's governing body, otherwise than by the LEA, to ensure that the school preserves its particular religious character or that it is conducted in accordance with the terms of a trust deed (or, if a school has neither religious character nor a trust deed, is appointed as a foundation governor).

Foundation school – a school introduced by the School Standards and Framework Act 1998. Totally funded by an LEA. The governing body employ the staff and control student admissions.

Foundation Stage – The curriculum provided for children aged 3, 4 and 5 wherever they are – includes children in nursery and reception classes in schools. Requires both indoor and outdoor play to be available all day.

Fresh Start – Describes the re-opening of a school closed after being found to be failing, usually under new leadership and with a new name.

GCSE – General Certificate of Secondary Education examinations taken at the end of Key Stage 4.

Gifted – programmes for students of exceptional ability. Services include pull-out programmes, in-class programmes and accelerated courses. Teaching content stresses concepts, problem-solving and higher level thinking skills.

GNVQ – General National Vocational Qualification – a vocational qualification at 16 plus concentrating on a broad area of work such as business, manufacturing, health and social care.

(former) Grant-maintained school – a primary or secondary school previously financed through the Funding Agency for Schools (FAS) after parents had voted to opt out of LEA control.

HMI – Her Majesty's Inspectorate of Schools.

HOD – Head of Department e.g. Head of English

HOY – Head of Year e.g. Head of Year 7.

Human Rights Act 1998 – States that it is unlawful for organisations, including schools and governing bodies, to act in a way that infringes the rights and freedoms of any person (adults and children) guaranteed under the European Convention for the Protection of Human Rights and Fundamental Freedoms.

IEP – Individual Education Plan for students with special educational needs

Independent School – private, not part of a municipal or state system. However, independent schools may contract with public systems to provide services.

In-service Education and Training (INSET) – the professional training and development of teachers working in schools – generally taken as short courses or day conferences.

Instrument of Government – legal document providing for the composition of a governing body of a school.

I(C)T – Information (and Communication) Technology.

IIP – Investors in People – a national accreditation which recognises effective systems, staff support and development structures in a business or organisation (such as a school).

Key Stages – the four stages of students' progress in acquiring knowledge and skills as set out in the National Curriculum. Students are tested at the end of each stage. Key Stage 1 where the majority of students are aged 5 to 7, Key Stage 2 where most are aged 8 to 11, Key Stage 3 where most are aged 12 to 14, and Key Stage 4 where most are aged 15 to 16.

Lay member – a member appointed to a panel hearing appeals against non-admission or exclusion, being a person without personal experience in managing or providing education in any school (other than as a governor or on a voluntary basis). He or she must not have, or have had, any connection with the school, or any person who is a member of, or employed by, the governing body if that might raise doubts about his or her ability to act fairly.

LEA – Local Education Authority. A local government body responsible for providing education for children of school age in a particular area.

LEA-maintained schools – schools for which LEAs have financial and administrative responsibility.

Local Management of Schools (LMS) – the term that describes a scheme for delegating financial responsibility from the LEA to schools.

LSA – learning support assistant, also called classroom assistant.

LSS – Learning Support Service.

Maintained school – see LEA-maintained school.

NAHT – National Association of Headteachers.

National Curriculum – the curriculum laid down by law for all children aged from 5 to 16 in state schools. This was established by the 1988 Education Reform Act to ensure that all students receive a broad and balanced education which is relevant to their needs.

NGfL – National Grid for Learning. A scheme to increase the level of ICT equipment in schools, to connect all schools to the Internet, and to bring to teachers and learners the benefits of on-line communication and services.

Non-teaching staff – members of school staff employed by the governors to provide services in a school other than teaching, such as classroom or learning support assistants and school secretaries.

NLS – National Literacy Strategy.

NNS – National Numeracy Strategy.

NQT – newly qualified teacher.

NUT – National Union of Teachers.

Office for Standards in Education (Ofsted) – the body which arranges and sets standards for school inspections.

Open enrolment – all schools must admit students up to their standard number (see PAN) which is calculated according to the physical capacity of the school to accommodate students.

Outturn – statement of what the school actually spent by the end of the financial year.

PAN – Planned Admissions Number – the number of children the LEA (or governing body of an Aided School) determines can be admitted to the school. Parents decide whether to appeal to any school to which they have applied and not been offered a place.

PANDA – Performance and Assessment Report – profile of the school provided annually by Ofsted containing a range of comparative and contextual performance data (Not applicable to special schools).

Parent – includes any person having all the rights, duties, powers, responsibility and authority (see Parental Responsibility) which a parent of a child has by law, or who has care of him or her. Depending on the circumstances, therefore, a 'parent' may include not only the child's natural parents but also others such as step-parents, relatives, co-habitees of either natural parent and foster parents.

Parent governor – a parent elected by other parents of children at a school to serve on the school's governing body.

Parental responsibility – all the rights, duties, powers, responsibilities and authority which a parent of a child has by law. More than one person may have parental responsibility for the same child at the same time, and a person does not cease to have such responsibility solely because some other person subsequently also acquires it. Both parents have parental responsibility if they were married to each other at the time of the child's birth, even if they have since separated or divorced. If the child's parents were not married at the time of the birth, the mother always has parental responsibility and the father may have by agreement or by order of the Court. Parental responsibility passes to the adopter when an adoption order is made. Although a residence order or care order may confer parental responsibility, a local authority will not be treated as a parent for certain purposes under the Education Acts.

PAT – Professional Association of Teachers.

Peripatetic teacher – one who gives specialist instruction in a number of schools, for example in music.

PGCE – Post-Graduate Certificate of Education. A teaching qualification.

PGR – Parent Governor Representative – elected by parent governors to a LEA Education Committee (since June 2000).

PICSI – Pre-Inspection Context and School Information contextual school information published by Ofsted before an inspection.

PRP – Performance Related Pay.

PSE (PSHE) – Personal and Social/Personal, Social and Health Education – includes issues such as sex education, drugs awareness, citizenship in primary schools. In secondary schools citizenship education is a separate subject, statutory since September 2002.

PTA/PSA – Parent Teacher Association – or PSA (Parent School Association).

PTR – Student/Teacher ratio.

Public private partnership (PPP) – The introduction of private sector funding and expertise into the provision of public services in order to achieve best value for money for taxpayers.

Students on roll – students registered at a school.

QCA – Qualifications and Curriculum Authority – has responsibility for curriculum matters. Produces schemes of work including the National Curriculum, assessments, , GNVQS, GCSEs etc.

QTS – Qualified Teacher Status

Quorum – the number of governors who must be present to validate the proceedings of a governors' meeting.

Race Relations (Amendment) Act 2000 – Schools are required to monitor the attainment of ethnic minority students and have a race equality policy with procedures for recording and dealing with racist incidents. Ofsted inspections have to report on how a school prevents and addresses racism and ensures racial equality.

Regulations – Subordinate legislation deriving its authority from an Act of Parliament, legally binding on governing bodies and others (see also Statutory Instrument).

Resolution – A proposal made formally at a meeting which has been voted on and agreed.

RGI/RI – Registered Inspector, who is authorised to lead an Ofsted inspection team (colloquially, a 'Reggie').

School Causing Concern – Under the LEA: Schools Code of Practice an LEA may send a warning letter to and require an action plan from a school where standards are unacceptably low or at risk of dropping further.

School Curriculum and Assessment Authority (SCAA) – Body corporate responsible for reviewing and advising the Secretary of State for Education and Employment on the school curriculum.

School Organisation Committee (SOC/SOP) – Required to be established by the LEA to consider its School Organisation Plan (SOP) for the provision of school places in its area.

School Standards and Framework Act 1998 (SSFA) – A significant piece of legislation setting out the government's aims and agenda for education.

School Teachers Review Body (STRB) – A body appointed by the Prime Minister to examine and report on such matters relating to the statutory conditions of employment of school teachers including teachers' pay.

SEN and Disability Act 2001 – Requires schools to ensure that they are accessible to and do not discriminate against anyone with a disability. The government will be providing guidance and funding over three years from 2002.

SENCO – Special Educational Needs (see below) Co-ordinator. The teacher responsible for co-ordination SEN provision in the school.

Serious Weaknesses – A school that is not failing may still have serious weaknesses, as identified in an Ofsted inspection. Action is required to make improvements within one year.

Service Level Agreement (SLA) – Document provided by the LEA to schools describing the services offered centrally. Schools can agree to 'buy in' or go elsewhere for any particular service e.g. Personnel; Finance; Schools Library Service.

Senior Management Team (SMT)

Setting – A system of organising students into ability groups for particular subjects.

Single regeneration budget (SRB) – Funding for projects undertaken in co-operation with education, health, community and business partners aimed at improving standards.

Special Agreement School – type of voluntary school that owes its existence to pre-1941 agreements between the Government and voluntary bodies.

Special education needs (SEN) – A child is defined as having Special Educational Needs if he or she has a learning difficulty which needs special teaching. A learning difficulty means that the child has significantly greater difficulty in learning than most children of the same age.

Special Measures – A judgement by Ofsted that a school requires special measures. These have to be identified in an Action Plan drawn up by the head-teacher and governing body in conjunction with the LEA to address the school's weaknesses. The LEA provides support and funding. The school is visited each term by inspectors to determine progress made.

Specialist Schools – A government programme for schools offering a broadly balanced curriculum, but with an emphasis on a chosen specialisation.

Special school – A school for children whose special educational needs cannot be met within a mainstream school.

Special unit – A unit attached to a mainstream school to cater for children with specific special needs.

Standard Assessment Tasks (SATs) – National tests/tasks set by SCAA.

Standards Fund – Funds mostly devolved to schools for specific purposes such as support for school management and governor support.

Standard number (SN) – The number of places available at a maintained (other than special) school for students of any age group in which they are admitted. The standard number is an indicator of the school's physical capacity to accommodate students. The school's admission authority may fix a different admission number which may be higher but not lower than the standard number.

Standard Spending Assessment (SSA) – The minimum standard level of public spending in each local authority determined by the government.

Standing Advisory Council on Religious Education (SACRE) – Committee advising an LEA on matters connected with Religious education and collective worship in schools. Local churches and other faith communities and teachers are represented.

Statement – A statement issued, after an assessment, for a child with significant learning difficulties which describes the help the child needs and the appropriate school s/he should attend. The statement is drawn up in consultation with parents and funded by the LEA.

Statement of special educational needs – A written statement of a child's special educational needs and all the extra help he or she should get. The arrangements are made by the LEA.

Statutory Assessment – The process, undertaken by the LEA, of assessing a child to determine whether or not s/he needs a statement of special educational needs.

Statutory Instrument (SI) – Subordinate legislation made under the authority of an Act of Parliament, usually authorised by the Secretary of State or one of his/her ministerial team, and which is normally laid before Parliament. It has the same force in law as an Act of Parliament.

Streaming – Placing students in classes according to their ability.

Support Staff – Clerical, welfare, technical, caretaking or supervisory staff in schools.

Suspension – A process where a member of staff is told to stop working at the school temporarily, usually while a problem involving him or her is being investigated.

Targets – Governing bodies are responsible for setting and publishing targets for student achievement in English and Maths at the end of Key Stage 2 and in public exams in Key Stage 4. Additional targets may also be set, e.g. for attendance and exclusions. The LEA must also publish authority wide targets in these areas in its Education Development Plan.

Teacher Education Day (TED) – Each year five days during term time are set aside for staff training (INSET). Students do not attend school on these days.

Trust deed – The deed by which a Voluntary Aided school has been established.

Vertical grouping – Classes formed (in primary schools) with children of different age groups.

Vocational education – Instruction that prepares a student for employment immediately after completing secondary school. Although often thought of in terms of auto-shop or carpentry courses, such programmes frequently also include a strong academic component and teach such cutting-edge skills as computer-aided design.

Voluntary Aided (VA) – A school set up and owned by a voluntary body, usually a church, largely financed through an LEA. The governing body employs the staff and controls student admissions and religious education.

Voluntary controlled school – A school set up by a voluntary body, usually a church body (generally Church of England). Totally funded by an LEA. The LEA employs the staff.

Work experience – A planned programme as part of careers education which enables students in school time to sample experience of a working environment of their choice.

YOT – Youth Offenders Team.

Contacts

GTC Teachers' Qualifications
Section at 3rd Floor,
Cannon House, 24 The Priory
Queensway,
Birmingham B4 6BS
Tel: 0870 010 308.
www.gtce.org.uk

Home Office,
Immigration and Nationality
Directorate,
Block C, Whitgift Centre,
Wellesley Road,
Croydon CR9 1AT
Tel: 0870 606 7766

Student Support Helpline
0800 731 9133,
www.dfes.gov.uk/studentsupport

Teacher Training Agency (TTA)
Teaching information line
Tel: 0845 600 0991
www.canteach.gov.uk

Special helpline for teachers who
have trained and qualified outside
the UK
Tel: 0118 952 3966

UK National Academic Recognition
Information Centre (UK NARIC).
Oriel House,
Oriel Road,
Cheltenham, GL50 1XP,
Tel: 0124 226 0010
Fax:0124 225 8611,
e-mail: naric@ecctis.co.uk
www.naric.org.uk

Work Permits (UK)
5th Floor, Moorfoot,
Sheffield S1 4PQ
Tel: 011 425 94074
www.workpermits.gov.uk

Supply Teaching Agencies of the Recruitment and Employment Confederation

It would be unethical and unwise to recommend any particular supply teacher agency. The following have been selected as a starting point for finding a suitable supply teachers agency as they are members of the Recruitment and Employment Confederation that has a Code of Practice to set out clearly the responsibilities of employment businesses providing teachers and support staff to LEAs and schools in both the public and private sector. These are regularly updated at www. rec.uk.com

North West

ACADEMY SUPPLY AGENCY
FOURTH FLOOR, 1 UNION
COURT, COOK STREET,
LIVERPOOL, L2 4SJ
Name: MS KATE BIRMINGHAM
Tel: 0151 284 6778
Fax: 0151 284 6400
Email: kateb@academy.locall.net

EDUCATIONAL SUPPORT SVCS
(ESS)
394 EDGE LANE, FAIRFIELD,
LIVERPOOL, MERSEYSIDE,
L7 9QE
Name: MR J WILLIAMS
Tel: 0151 230 4000
Fax: 0151 230 4040

SUPPLYNET
1ST FLOOR, STARKIE COURT, 13
STARKIE STREET PRESTON,
LANCASHIRE, PR1 3LU
Name: MR M EDMONSON
Tel: 0177 256 3737
Fax: 0177 256 3740
Email: mark@supplynet.org.uk

PREMIER EDUCATION
3rd FLOOR, 82 KING STREET,
MANCHESTER, M2 4WQ
Name: MS CLARE PARRY
Tel: 0161 935 8117
Fax: 0161 935 8227
Email: clare@premier-education.
co.uk

East

ADVANTAGE EDUCATION
49 LODGE LANE, GRAYS,
ESSEX, RM17 5RZ
Name: ANDREW HARRISON
Tel: 0137 539 0888
Fax: 0137 554 5651
Email: teachers@advantage
education.com

MARK EDUCATION LIMITED
THE LIMES, 32-34 UPPER
MARLBOROUGH NEL, ST
ALBANS, HERTFORDSHIRE,
AL1 3UU
Name: MS S WRIGHT
Tel: 0172 781 2333
Fax: 0172 781 2409
Email: susan.wright@thelimes.com

SELECT EDUCATION
OPERATIONS MANAGER,
REGENT COURT, LAPORTE WAY,
LUTON, BEDFORDSHIRE,
LU4 8SB
Name: MS H HARVEY
Tel: 0158 281 1600
Email: h.harvey@select.co.uk

SELECT EDUCATION
REGENT COURT, LAPORTE WAY,
LUTON BEDFORDSHIRE,
LU4 8SB
Name: MR R WICKS
Tel: 0158 240 6800
Fax: 0158 281 1736
Email: b.wicks@select.co.uk

TEACHERS UK
1 WELLS YARD, HIGH STREET,
WARE, HERTFORDSHIRE,
SG12 9AS
Name: MR L BRESSLAW
Tel: 0192 048 4428
Fax: 0192 048 6692

TEACHING PEOPLE
10 – 10a DUNSTABLE PLACE,
LUTON, BEDFORDSHIRE,
LU1 2QT
Name: MR N HOPPER
Tel: 0158 248 8972
Fax: 0158 248 8922

TEACHING PERSONNEL LTD
PERSONNEL HOUSE, 99 BRIDGE
ROAD EAST, WELWYN GARDEN
CITY, HERTFORDSHIRE, AL7 19L
Name: MS FIONA ELDRIDGE
Tel: 0800 015 7833
Fax: 0170 738 6386
Email: fiona.eldridge@teaching
personnel.com
www.teachingpersonnel.com
TOPLINE STAFF SERVICES
11 BRIDGE STREET, LEIGHTON
BUZZARD, BEDFORDSHIRE,
LU7 1AH
Name: MS S GANT
Tel: 0152 537 3098
Fax: 0152 537 0136

North East
CAPSTAN TEACHERS
WALSH COURT, 10 BELLS
SQUARE, TRIPPET LANE,
SHEFFIELD, SOUTH
YORKSHIRE, S1 2FY
Name: MS A BUSHNELL
Tel: 0114 276 3591
Fax: 0114 276 3592

FOCUS EDUCATION
THE OLD VETERINARY
SURGERY, 6A QUEEN STREET,
NEWCASTLE, STAFFORDSHIRE,
ST5 1ED
Name: MIKE REES-BOUGHTON
Tel: 0178 261 1991
Fax: 0178 262 1885
Email: mike@focuseducation.net
Web site: www.focuseducation.net

STAFFLEX LTD
93 WAKEFIELD ROAD, ASPLEY,
HUDDERSFIELD, HD5 9AN
Name: MR PAUL BALDERSTONE
Tel: 0148 435 1010
Fax: 0148 435 1020
Email: staff@stafflex.co.uk

STANDBY TEACHER SERVICES
LTD
46A THE GROVE, IILKLEY,
WEST YORKSHIRE, LS29 9EE
Name: MRS L SANDERSON –
PYRAH
Tel: 0194 386 4677
Fax: 0194 386 4353
Email: info@standbyteachers.com
Web site: www.standbyteachers.com

SUPPLY DESK LTD
GLOBE WORKS, PENISTONE
ROAD, SHEFFIELD, SOUTH
YORKSHIRE, S6 3AE
Name: MR S PETHERBRIDGE
Tel: 0114 201 1400
Fax: 0114 201 1401
Email: steve@thesupplydesk.co.uk

South West
ELEVATIONS OPPORTUNITY
LTD
14 CAMBRIAN ROAD,
NEWPORT, GWENT, NP20 4AB
Name: MR M SHEEHAN
Tel: 0163 376 2333
Fax: 0163 376 2444

MILLENNIUM PERSONNEL SVS
EDUCA
1ST FLOOR, 15 ELY VALLEY
ROAD, TALBOT GREEN,
RHONDDA, CYNON, TAFF,
CF72 8AL
Name: MRS Y PETERS
Tel: 0144 323 0222
Fax: 0144 323 0293

MILLENNIUM PERSONNEL
SERVICES
1ST FLOOR, 15 ELY VALLEY
ROAD, TALBOT GREEN,
RHONDDA, CYNON, TAFF,
CF72 8AL
Name: MR C HENSON
Tel: 0144 368 2266
Fax: 0144 368 8048

NEW DIRECTIONS (REC) LTD
ROYAL LONDON HOUSE, 28 ST
MARY STREET, CARDIFF,
WALES, CF10 1AB
Name: MR L TUNE
Tel: 0292 039 0150
Fax: 0292 039 0134

Midlands
EDUCATION STAFFING LINK
LTD
1489 PERSHORE ROAD,
STIRCHLEY, BIRMINGHAM,
WEST MIDLANDS, B30 2JL
Name: MRS D DAKIN
Tel: 0121 486 1985
Fax: 0121 459 8898
Email: support@est.uk.net
www.est.uk.net

EUROTEMP
37 GREENHILL STREET,
STRATFORD- UPON-AVON,
WARWICKSHIRE CV37 6LE
Name: MR CHRISTOPHER POUST
Tel: 0178 972 1115
Fax: 0178 972 0983
Email: info@eurotemprecruitment.com
Web site: www.eurotemprecruitment.com

GB RECRUITMENT (STAFFS) LTD
59 HARLEY STREET, HANLEY,
STOKE ON TRENT, ST1 3LB
Name: MR C S MARRIOTT
Tel: 0178 220 2626
Fax: 0178 226 2600
Email: info@gbrs.co.uk
Web site: www.gbrs.co.uk

MARK EDUCATION LTD
REGENT HOUSE, BATH
AVENUE, WOLVERHAMPTON,
WEST MIDLANDS, WV1 4EG
Name: MS S BULLOCK
Tel: 0190 257 6511
Fax: 0190 257 6514

MARK EDUCATION LIMITED
1ST FLOOR, 104-106 COLMORE
ROW, BIRMIMGHAM, WEST
MIDLANDS, B3 3AF
Name: MRS F PALMER
Tel: 0121 236 6674
Fax: 0121 236 2641

PLATO TEACHERS
CLOVER HOUSE, 4 MARY ROAD,
STECHFORD, BIRMINGHAM,
B33 8AP
Name: MR STEPHEN ROBINSON
Tel: 0121 628 5527
Fax: 0121 603 0646
Email: enquiries@platoteachers.com

PRIME TIME RECRUITMENT
ORIEL HOUSE, 55-57 SHEEP
STREET, NORTHAMPTON, NN1
2NE
Name: MR DARREN HAWKINS
Tel: 0160 460 2700
Fax: 0160 423 2499
Email: darren.hawkins@primetime.co.uk

STRATEGIC MOVES
EDUCATION RECRUITMENT
8TH FLOOR, COMMERCIAL
UNION HOUSE, 24 MARTINEAU
SQUARE, BIRMINGHAM,
B2 4UU
Name: MS MICHAELA POWELL
Tel: 0870 708 4033
Fax: 0870 708 4035
Email: kay@strategicmoves.com

South
ABACUS PROFESSIONALS
11 ABBOTSBURY ROAD,
MORDEN, SURREY, SM4 5LJ
Name: MRS P K EVANS
Tel: 0208 646 1001
Fax: 0208 648 1016

P & D EMPLOYMENT
5 CITY ROAD, WINCHESTER,
HAMPSHIRE, SO23 8SD
Name: MRS PENNY GOATER
Tel: 0196 286 5152
Fax: 0196 284 1674

WEST COUNTRY EDUCATIONAL
AGY
1 CANON SQUARE,
MELKSHAM, WILTSHIRE,
SN12 6LX
Name: MRS A BENHAM-TAYLOR
Tel: 0122 570 6726
Fax: 0122 570 6698
Email: staff@edagency.freeserve.
co.uk

London

A S A EDUCATION
GLADE HOUSE, 52 CARTER
LANE, LONDON, LONDON,
EC4Y 9EA
Name: MR D EDWARDS
Tel: 0207 236 4624
Fax: 0207 489 8494

CAPITA BUSINESS SERVICES
MERIDIAN HOUSE, ROYAL
HILL, GREENWICH, LONDON,
SE10 8RG
Name: MS M ROBINS
Tel: 0208 293 6318
Fax: 0208 858 8885

CASTLE RECRUITMENT LTD
618A ROMFORD ROAD, MANOR
PARK, LONDON, LONDON,
E12 5AQ
Name: MR A STEPAN
Tel: 0208 514 3888
Fax: 0208 514 3999
Email: andy@castlerecruitment.com

CFBT THE TEACHING AGENCY
6 LAMPTON ROAD, HOUNSLOW,
MIDDLESEX, TW3 1JL
Name: MS T MCNULTY
Tel: 0208 814 8200
Fax: 0208 814 8209
Email: teachingagency@cfbt-
hq.org.uk

EDUCATION VIP'S
50 HIGH STREET, BROMLEY,
KENT, BR1 1EG
Name: MS SYLVIA SNIPP
Tel: 0208 289 6487
Fax: 0208 289 6485
Email: post@educationvips.com
Web site: www.educationvips.com

GABBITAS EDUCATIONAL
CONSULTANTS
CARRINGTON HOUSE, 126-130
REGENT STREET, LONDON,
LONDON, W1R 6EE
Name: MISS J BRYER
Tel: 0207 734 0161
Fax: 0207 437 1764

LONG TERM TEACHERS LTD
26 MORTIMER STREET,
LONDON, W1N 7RA
Name: MR LOUISE POWELL
Tel: 0207 436 4949
Fax: 0207 436 4979
Email: louisepowell@longterm
teachers.com

MASTERLOCK RECRUITMENT
MAcMILLAN HOUSE, 96
KENSINGTON HIGH STREET,
LONDON, LONDON, W8 4SG
Name: MS D LONGSTAFF
Tel: 0207 938 1718
Fax: 0207 376 1704
Email: pauline@education.master
lock.co.uk

RECRUIT EDUCATION
SERVICES
5TH FLOOR, NEW ZEALAND
HOUSE, 80 HAYMARKET,
LONDON, LONDON, SW1Y 4TE
Name: MS R CROSS
Tel: 0207 930 4932
Fax: 0207 930 4994

SANZA TEACHING AGENCY
UNIT 3A, THE GALLERIA, 180-
182 GEORGE LANE, SOUTH
WOODFORD, LONDON, E18 1AY
Name: MR ASHLEY HARRIS
Tel: 0208 491 8368
Fax: 0208 491 8382
Email: ashley@teachuk.co.uk
Web site: www.teachuk.co.uk

SELECT EDUCATION
SALISBURY HOUSE, LONDON
WALL, LONDON, EC2M 5QQ
Name: MS ALEXANDRA KAIN
Tel: 0207 638 1849
Fax: 0207 638 1626

TATE & ASSOCIATES
1 GREENHILL RENTS, LONDON,
EC1M 6BN
Name: MR DAVID TATE
Tel: 0207 490 7049
Fax: 0207 490 7249
Email: tate.assoc@btinternet.com

TEACHERS 'R' US LTD
22 COLLEGE PARADE,
SALUSBURY ROAD, LONDON,
LONDON, NW6 6RN
Name: MS S ANKETILL
Tel: 0207 328 0000
Fax: 0207 328 0303

VERITY EDUCATION
47 SOUTH MOLTON STREET,
LONDON, LONDON, W1Y 1DF
Name: MR R HOWARD
Tel: 0207 629 8786
Fax: 0207 629 8828

Index